Offi

Charmanie Saquea

Chapter 1

Mykell

"That's how you feel? You just gon turn your back on me after all I've done for you? Really, Mykell?" I just kept walking. "Mykell! Don't fucking keep walking away from me. You know what, go to hell!" Neicey yelled.

I wanted to go back but I couldn't. The fact that I couldn't hold her and console her made me weak. Let the truth be told, I'm not even mad at her, I'm mad at myself. Mad that I even let her put herself in this situation. Every damn time we are going good, some bullshit pops up and sets us back. I've barely been married a fucking week and I can't even be happy like a normal person is supposed to be.

I'm supposed to be meeting up with Lakey to go see this lawyer he wants to hire for Neicey. His name is Toni Hunt. Lakey checked his credentials and he is supposed to be a real fucking bad ass. I can tell by how much he is charging. I pulled up to Lakey's and blew for him to come out.

Two minutes later, he walked out the house. "Wassup man? How did it go?" he asked.

"Not good man, not good at all." I shook my head at the thought off Neicey flipping out on my ass. Her last words stung as I remembered them. *You know what, go to hell!*

I felt like shit for leaving her like that. She just didn't understand that is no place I want for my damn wife to be. Hell, I've been locked up before; I know what it's like. I hate for her to go through this shit. I would be lying if I said I didn't appreciate the fact that she turned herself in for me. Like seriously, I don't know any female that would do that for a nigga. This shit just proves just how much she's down for me and how much she loves me.

When we walked in the building of the lawyer's office, the shit was real fancy. The floors looked freshly polished, a big chandelier and all that extra shit. Lakey walked up to the receptionist's desk and asked for Toni Hunt.

Two minutes later we were allowed to go back. My jaw damn near hit the floor when I saw a caramel skinned cutie sitting behind the desk typing something on her computer. I looked over at Lakey and he looked just as shocked as me. She looked up at us and smiled. She had a cute set of dimples that reminded me of Neicey.

"Hello, I'm Toni," she said, getting up and walking over to shake our hands. Baby was stacked! She had on a black pantsuit with a pink dress shirt and pink pumps. Her ass was fat as hell. It's been a long time since I've even cared to look at another woman besides Neicey, but baby girl was bad.

"I'm Mykell Jones and this is Lashaun Mitchell," I said, shaking her hand.

"Alright Mr. Jones, what can I do for you gentlemen?"

Lakey spoke up this time. "Well we need a lawyer for my best friend and his wife."

I saw a wake of shock flash over her eyes when Lakey said "wife."

"So, what are the charges we're looking at?" she asked.

"Right now, it could be two charges of murder," I spoke up.

"Wow, okay so what happened?" she said, getting a pen and notebook out.

"Yesterday, we were coming back from our honeymoon in the D.R. when two police officers came to arrest me for the murders. At the station, before I could even get questioned, I was told I was free to go. They never told me why but I later found out that my wife confessed to the murders....without a lawyer present," I said, filling her in.

"So your wife, what's her name?" she said.

"Reneice."

"Okay, so Reneice turned herself in for the murders that you were originally a suspect in?" she said, like she couldn't believe it.

"Pretty much," I said.

"Hmm...Alright I'll go see her today and see what I can find out. That is, if she's willing to talk to me."

"She will," Lakey and I answered at the same time

"I'll be keeping in touch," she said, eyeing me, and I could tell that had a double meaning to it.

Lakey

I could remember a time when Neicey had sworn off men. Now, she was getting her ass locked up and more for a nigga. This shit was so shocking. I always knew she was loyal but she just took the meaning of that word to a whole new level.

"Man, spark that shit up," Mykell said, tossing me a blunt and lighter once we got in the car.

"You ain't gotta ask me twice," I said.

By the time I got it lit, my phone was ringing.

"You have a collect call from Neicey," the automated system said.

I pressed 0 and waited to hear her voice. "Hello," she said.

"Yo Snook! Wassup?"

"Hey Lakey, what you doing?" she asked.

"Shit, just left from seeing this lawyer we hired for yo stubborn ass. She said she gon come through to see you sometime today."

"She?"

"Yea man, be nice too. I paid a lot of money for her to represent yo ass."

"I guess. How my babies doing?"

"They doing good. You already know MyMy running shit like it's her house," I laughed.

"Just like her mama," she chuckled.

I looked over at Kell and he was smoking that damn blunt like it was his last. "I'm with yo husband," I said, noticing not one time did she ask about him. "Wanna holla at him?" I asked.

"Not really. I don't have shit to say to him."

"Oh, alright. Well Imma try to come see you later on this week."

"Okay. Give my kids a hug and kiss and let them know I love them."

"You know I got you."

After we hung up, I looked at Mykell wondering what the fuck was going on with them.

"What y'all into it about now?" I asked.

"Man, I went to see her and shit went all bad." He sighed. "I said some shit I didn't mean and we exchanged some words. Yo Lake, you just don't know that this shit is killing me. My wife, not my girl, but my fuckin *wife,* is sitting behind bars because of some shit I did and the part that's killing me the most is the fact that I don't even know how the hell the police found out about this shit," he said, rubbing his hand over his head.

"Don't trip bruh; this shit is just a minor setback for a major comeback. We gon bring her home, no doubt about it. But now is not the time for y'all to be falling apart. Just like you need her, she really needs you. I can just imagine how she's feeling right now, especially since she's never been locked up before," I said.

"You're right man, let's just forget all the bullshit and worry about bringing my baby home. You know her lil stubborn ass is just mad right now, she'll come around"

"You know it." I laughed.

Reneice

I'm not even gon lie or try to front; I was fuckin hurt after Mykell left here. It seems like every time we make progress, we always get set back. He was mad because I covered for his ass? Where they do that at? Now Lakey was talking about my damn lawyer was a female and his ass knew I didn't get along with chicks. On top of that, I was missing my kids, especially my little diva. I know she had to be giving her daddy hell because she acts just like me.

They got me in this cold ass room waiting to see what this lawyer chick is about. After waiting a few minutes, she finally walked in. She extended her hand for me to shake.

"Mrs. Jones, I'm Toni Hunt. Your friend and husband hired me to work your case," she said.

I shook her hand.

She looked at me for a minute then tilted her head to the side like she was trying to figure something out. "So Reneice, how long have you and Mykell been together?" she asked.

What the fuck is up with her and this first name basis shit? I thought to myself.

"Why?"

"I'm just trying to figure out why you would turn yourself in for him, that's all."

"Because I wanted to," I said, keeping it short with her ass.

"Hmm," she said, reaching into her brief case. "I stopped and picked up some papers and by looking at your confession, I can get you off on self-defense," she said, looking at some papers.

"So when do I go to trial?" I asked, ready for this shit to be all over.

"Well, you have a bail hearing Monday morning at 9:00. I will ask for a speedy trial."

"I guess." I sighed.

"Alright, I will keep in touch with you and feel free to contact me whenever you need to," she said, handing me a card.

* * *

Later on that week, I was in my cell just staring up at the ceiling. *Was this shit even worth it? I have only been in here two days and my so called husband has already turned his back on me.*

"Jones," the guard said, shaking me from my thoughts. "You have a visitor," he said.

When I got to the visiting room, I saw Lakey and I smiled.

"Wassup Snook, you ain't dropped the soap yet have you?" he laughed.

"Don't be funny nigga," I said laughing with him.

"Naw, but for real, how you holding up?" he asked.

"I'm good, considering the fact that they denied my bail," I shrugged. "How my babies doing?"

"They doing good, your daughter is bossy as she can be." He looked at me seriously. "You haven't talked to them?"

"I talked to MJ the other day; he told me everybody was good."

"What about Kell?" he asked.

"What about him?" I said.

"C'mon now Reneice, don't be like that."

"Like what? I'm in here because of him but he turned his back on me," I said with my voice shaking with emotion.

"That man did not turn his back on you. Was he not there at your bail hearing? Did he not go half on a lawyer for you?" he asked.

"Yea, but he also said I was stupid for what I did and basically said I would not see my kids as long as I'm in here."

He sighed. "Look Snook, Imma keep it real with you. Mykell is hurting just as bad as you are. You have to look at it from his point. Imma break it down for you in a man's perspective. How do you think he feels about his wife sitting behind bars for him? Neicey you turned yourself in and admitted to doing some shit that he was originally arrested for. Do you know how he feels right now?" he asked.

I just shook my head no.

"Well, Imma tell you. He feels like he's not a damn man. His job is to protect his family by all means and make sure you and his kids are straight. Instead of him protecting you, you're protecting him. He feels fucking worthless right now, especially since there's nothing he can do about it."

Damn, I thought. "Alright, I understand now. But what I need him to understand was I took my wedding vows seriously. I wouldn't have dare done some crazy shit like this if I wasn't sure that I could walk away free from this. Toni got some documents from the hospital concerning the condition I was in when I got there. So everything is looking pretty good right now," I said.

"That's wassup big head." He smiled. "I need you to get out so you can meet this little female I met."

"Aw shoot, my old boo is falling in love." I smiled.

"Nah, I wouldn't say all that," he laughed.

"Well, it gotta be something if you want me to meet her."

"I'm feeling her, I'm feeling her a lot, but you know I need you to check her out and shit for me," he said.

"I got you."

"Yo, call ya husband," he said.

"I will, I promise."

We ended our visit and I went back to my cell to do some more thinking. I came to the conclusion that it is most definitely worth it.

Chapter 2

Ramone

Neicey wasn't the only one dealing with some shit right now. My life was all messed up right now, a complete mess. The woman I gave my heart to and I are not together anymore and I don't get see my daughter as much as I would like. I remember the day my life changed for the worst.

Le'Lani, Zamier, and I were in the hospital for 10 hours. Her water broke but the baby was too stubborn to come out. Finally, at 6:00 in the morning, she was ready to push.

"I see the head, one more big push for me," the doctor aid.

"Ahhhhh!" Lani screamed as she pushed.

"We have a baby girl," the doctor announced.

I looked at Lani and could tell that she was tired.

"Umm, is there a way we can do a DNA test since she's here?" Zamier asked.

I looked at him like he was crazy. Damn, the baby was just born and he already wanna do the test. What's the rush?

"That's fine with me, if it's okay with her mother" the doctor said.

I looked over at Lani, she just shrugged her shoulders. "I guess," she said faintly.

"Okay, who wants to go first?" the doctor asked.

"He can go first," I spoke up.

"Alright."

A week later, the results came back that I was not the father. Ever since that day, my and Lani's relationship hasn't been the same. I know I did all that talking about how I would be there for her and the baby no matter what, but I let my pride get in the way and I eventually ended up pushing her away. We started fighting and arguing over dumb stuff. She finally got fed up and left, taking my daughter with her, and I didn't even try to stop her.

We've been broken up almost for a year and I would be lying if I said I didn't still love her or miss her, but that shit was just too much to handle. I was in the car headed to Pops' house to get my daughter for the weekend. When I pulled up to his house, I saw his car, Lani's car and a car that I didn't recognize.

I knocked on the door and waited for an answer. A minute later, Pops opened up the door.

"Wassup Pops?" I greeted my second father.

"Nothing, nothing at all," he said, shaking his head.

I looked around the living room and saw boxes everywhere. Before I could even speak on it, my daughter came running around the corner.

"Daddyyyyy!" Ranyla screamed as she jumped in my arms.

"Hey princess, I missed you," I said, kissing her all over her face.

"I miss you more," she giggled.

I looked up when I saw Lani coming down the stairs carrying a box with Zamier behind her.

"Mommy, my daddy here," Ranyla announced.

Lani looked at me and gave me a weak smile. I noticed that her bitch ass baby daddy gave me the evil eye but I brushed it off and smirked.

"Wassup with all the boxes?" I asked.

"Um..."

Before she could even answer, Zamier spoke up. "She's moving," he said matter-of-factly.

"Is that right?"

"Yea."

Pops came back in the room and took Ranyla out my arms. "Zamier, I think you need to let them two have a minute to talk. Mone and Lani, go in the den, now," he said in a no nonsense tone.

I followed behind Lani to the den because we both knew that Pops wasn't playing with our asses.

"So wassup? You was gon move and not tell me nothing?" I asked while closing the door.

She stood on the other side of the room looking everywhere but at me. "I was going to tell you."

"Oh really?" I asked sarcastically. "So where you moving to?"

"With Zamier," she said in a low tone.

"Come again?" I said, as I walked towards her, which made her take two steps back. "So what? Y'all a fucking couple now? What's all that shit you was popping about not wanting to be with him?"

"He said he wanted to be close to his daughter without having to come pick her up from here, besides you don't want me no more, so why does it even matter?" she said, finally looking me in my eyes.

"So the fuck what!" I yelled. "I have to come pick my daughter up whenever the fuck you feel like letting me see her, so why the hell can't he do it?"

I couldn't believe she was in my face spitting this bullshit. Who the fuck is this, because this sure ain't the girl I fell in love with. *She can't be fucking serious.*

"I'll be by to pick up NyNy Sunday night," she said, acting like what I just said didn't mean shit.

"Speaking of, I don't want my daughter around that nigga. I don't know him like that to be trusting him around her 24/7," I said.

She looked at me like she was offended. "So what are you saying?"

"I'm saying, if you move in with that nigga, I'm taking you to court for custody of Ranyla; my daughter."

"Fuck you Ramone, that's my daughter!" she yelled.

"And? Don't you have another one? Since you wanna play house with that nigga, do it with y'all daughter because I'll be damned if you do it with mines."

She shook her head. "You ain't shit, after I treated *your* son like my own, welcomed him into *my* house, the same house yo as still laying up in…you know what, fuck it and you. See you in court muthafucka," she said, brushing past me and walking out the door.

I just shook my head and sat on the couch with my head in my hands, wondering how the hell we went from being in love to this bullshit.

"You know, I was once told if you love something, let it go," Pops said, walking in the room with Ranyla on his heels. "That's my daughter and I love her, but she has to learn from her own mistakes. Personally, I don't trust that nigga as far as I can throw him. I have bullets with his name on em as soon as he fucks up. I protected her all her life because she's my youngest child and my only daughter, but now the only thing I can do now is be there for her when she gets hurt."

"No offense or disrespect Pops, but your daughter is on some bullshit," I said as I watched my daughter play with her toys.

"It's not her, it's him. He just came in here the other day telling her that she needed to move in with him because he wasn't going to let another nigga raise his daughter."

"They're crazy as hell if they think I'm going to let my daughter live with them, I'll be damned."

"Daddy, I want ice cream and I want to see Keiyari," Ranyla said with her hands on her hips.

"You are too grown for me," I chuckled.

"Have you heard from your sister?" Pops asked.

"She called me the other day; apparently her and Kell are into it again. It seems like Micah and Janae are the only ones in a happy relationship," I said.

"All relationships go through stuff, but only real relationships make it through and come out strong," he said, standing up. "Now get out and go spend time with your daughter, I have a date." He laughed while leaving the room.

Lani

I couldn't believe Ramone had the audacity to tell me that he was going to take me to court for custody of Ranyla. It would be a cold day in hell before I let that happen. He had a lot of nerve trying to be mad at me when he was the one who turned his back on me. That nigga talked a good game while I was pregnant, talking about what he was gon do, but the moment we got the results, his ass folded.

That's crazy because I accepted Keiyari, treated him like he was my son and everything. I accepted the fact that he had a son before we got together but now he wanna act funny because I conceived a child with someone else when we were broken up. All I can do is shake my head. That's some bullshit. I guess he doesn't like it when the shoe is on the other foot.

"What's wrong with you?" Zamier asked as he drove.

"Nothing," I said.

"You sure? You seem real salty about something."

"I said I'm fine," I rolled my eyes.

I looked down at my vibrating phone, it was an unknown number but I answered anyway. "Hello."

"You have a collect call from, Neicey. If you wish to accept these charges, press zero."

"Hey mami!" I said after pressing zero.

"Wassup boo? What's going on?"

"Nothing really, just missing my crazy sister," I laughed.

"I miss you too. What my nieces doing?" she asked.

"Well, Zyla is sleeping and Ranyla is with her dad."

"Okay, well, give Zy kisses for me. So how you and knucklehead doing?"

"Good," I lied.

Neicey was locked up and had more important things to worry about instead of her brother's and my problems.

"Cut the bull, Le'Lani. I'm your sister so you don't have to lie to me. Mone already told me that y'all not together no more," she said, shocking me.

I sighed. "It's not that important Neicey, so don't even worry about it. The only thing that matters right now is getting you out of jail."

"I'm not worried about that right now, I'm wondering how you're feeling."

"I'm dealing with it the best way I know how. I mean it's really nothing I can do about it now."

"Alright boo, you know I'm still here for you even though I'm in a fucked up situation right now. No matter who you're with, you will always be my sister."

"I know. I'm coming to see you as soon as I finished getting settled in and stuff."

"Alright, you do that."

"Love you."

"Love you back."

My mind was in one place and my heart was in another. I would be lying if I said I didn't still love Ramone but he did me real foul. I took responsibility for my actions, so I guess there was nothing for me to do but put on my big girl panties and suck it up.

MJ

If it's not one thing, it's another. It seems like my mom and dad can never be happy for too long. Every time they get good, some shit always gotta happen to fuck them up. I was fifteen years old now and I peep shit even when they think I'm not paying attention. When ma was in the hospital, I thought I would never get to see her again. Now she's locked up and I feel the same way.

My dad is really lucky to have a woman in his life. She took me in and raised me as her own without any problems; she did the same with Tyriq. Not a lot of women would do some stuff like that. Even when they had broken up and she was with Kamil, I could tell that she still loved my dad. They have this crazy kind of love that only they and the people around them can understand.

One day, when I get serious and settle down, I want a woman like my mom; strong, independent, beautiful, loving, determined, smart and sophisticated. I had been kicking it with this girl I went to school with named Chyanne and she reminded me of my mom a little. She was beautiful and very smart; the good girl type, so I have to be very careful with her.

"Dad, how many times have you been in love?" I asked as we watched TV.

"One time, why?" he looked at me funny.

"I'm just wondering. Who was it?" I asked, even though I already I knew what the answer would be.

"The only person I gave my last name to, of course."

"So you mean to tell me all those years you were with that Kya chick you didn't love her? Seven years is a long time to be with somebody and not love them."

"I never said I didn't love her, I just wasn't in love with her. I was in love with the things she could do. She was more of a convenience for me."

"So when you met mom, how did you know you was in love with her and not just infatuated?"

"Imma tell you like yo Pop-Pop told me, if your heart flutters when you see her then it's love. But if she only makes your dick hard, it might just be lust. She made my heart flutter every time I seen her, even now it still flutters," he said, smiling.

"Sucka fa love." I laughed.

"Whatever lil nigga, wait until it happens to you, you'll understand then," he said, mushing me.

"I guess."

"So Mykell Jr., are you still a virgin?" he asked out of nowhere.

"Should I be a virgin?" I retorted.

"What a virgin daddy?" Amyricale asked from behind us.

"Something you better be for the rest of your life," he said, kissing her face as she climbed in his lap.

She giggled. "Silly daddy."

The house phone started to ring so I got up and answered it, shaking my head at my dad and sister.

"Hello?" I answered.

I got happy when I heard the operator speaking. I was happy to hear from my mom. I truly missed her.

"Hey ma, how you doing?" I said as soon as I pressed zero.

"Hey baby, I'm good. What you doing?"

"Sitting here with dad and MyMy." I said.

"Where's Fat Fat and Tyriq?" she asked.

"Upstairs in Romell's room."

"You keeping them out of trouble?"

"You know I am." I laughed.

"Alright, I love you. Let me talk to your dad real quick."

"Love, you too." I handed the phone to my dad and left the room.

"MJ," I heard from behind me.

"Wassup, Princess?" I said as I picked Amyricale up.

"Is Mommy coming home? Her no love me?" she said pouting.

"Of course mommy is coming home baby girl, and she loves you very much. She just has some stuff she has to get together."

"Sure?"

"I'm sure."

"Okay!" she perked up.

It hurt that my sister thought ma didn't love her anymore. She was taking it the worst out of all of us kids. I think it's because she doesn't really understand what's going on. Even Tyriq was taking it well, and he was her damn shadow when she was home. I was just ready for all this nonsense to be over.

Pop-Pop

These damn kids of mine were going to drive me crazy! Every day they found something else to stress me out about. I had one daughter behind bars, one daughter losing her mind behind her child's father, and a son trying to go through with a custody battle. What's next? I'm barely fifty years old and already got grey hairs. That's not acceptable. I don't know what the hell is wrong with these damn kids. I'll be happy when they get their shit together. I feel like I'm running a damn crazy house. It seems like every time I say something to them, it goes in one ear and out the other.

"Noah, what the hell we gon do about these damn kids?" Big Mone asked.

"Man, I don't even know." I shook my head.

He fixed himself a drink then sat in a chair in the den. "Who would have thought that we would be best friends as kids and teenagers, lose touch, then I come home and find out my daughter is dating your son."

I chuckled. "I knew the moment Le'Lani brought her home for me to meet her. I knew exactly who she was. So instantly I took her in as family. She looks just like Sharice."

"Doesn't she, it kind of scares me sometimes because she acts just like her too. But Le'Lani, that's Cherry all the way." He laughed.

"Tell me about, it's like another Cherry all over again." I shook my head. "We had some good girls though, Mone."

"Yes we did, which is why it should be no surprise our daughters are the way they are. They are their mothers' children."

"Yea, but it's just something's not right with this Zamier dude. I get a real funny feeling with him."

"He seems like the controlling type. I'm still trynna figure out how he just took Lani out of here and told her that she's moving in with him." He shook his head.

"Man, you should have seen the look on your son's face when he found out. I thought he was going to lose his mind."

"He handled it way better than I would have. I just don't agree with him trying to take her to court for custody of Ranyla though, that doesn't sit well with me because no matter what, Lani is a good mother."

"Yea but the only thing we can do is give them our advice, the choice is really up to them," I said.

"Yea, you're right," he agreed.

Hopefully they make the right choice.

Janae

For the past two weeks, I've been feeling like someone is watching me. I would tell Micah but he's already dealing with a lot with Neicey being locked up and he says Le'Lani has been acting funny lately; so the last thing I want to do is add on to his stress. Our relationship has been going great, minus the disagreements we have, but that's normal. Lil Mack looks more and more like his daddy every day. Ranee is still my mini-me. Whenever their dad walks into a room, they forget all about me. He has the both of them so spoiled.

"Mama, Lil Mack wants his bottle," Ranee said, walking into the kitchen.

"Where is it?" I asked.

"He left it in his car seat in the car."

Damn, I thought. "Alright, keep an eye on your brother while I go get it."

I walked outside to the driveway to grab his bottle. I noticed an all black Navigator across the street but thought nothing of it. *It's probably one of the neighbors.* I unlocked the door and reached in the backseat.

"Wassup Nae Nae, long time no see," I heard from behind me and instantly froze. I turned around and was face to face with the last person I expected to see.

"B-Bishop? What are you doing here? I thought you were locked up," I said, staring at my deceased ex-boyfriend's brother.

"Well not anymore, apparently."

"What do you want?" I asked as I glanced back towards the house. *I'm so happy Micah's not here.*

"You know what I want. How's my niece doing? Or should I say my daughter?" he asked with malice dripping from his voice.

My heart dropped and a lump formed in my throat.

"What are you talking about Bishop? Ranee is not your daughter; I don't know what would make you think that."

"Oh, you know why, don't play dumb with me Janae," Bishop said, walking closer to me.

"Mama!" I turned around to see my son standing there rubbing his eyes.

"Go back in the house baby; I'll be in there in a minute," I said.

"Okay," he said, running back in the house.

"Look Janae, you better stop playing with me and let me see my daughter."

"She's not your daughter Bishop! You know Rodney is her father."

"How would you know if you never got a DNA test done? Keep playing with me if you want to, you won't like the outcome," he said, walking back towards the navigator.

"Shit," I yelled as I ran back into the house, locking the door. I went straight to my bedroom, ignoring my kids in the process. I let out a breath I didn't even realize I was holding when I reached Micah's and my bedroom. I shook my head, deeply regretting the day wish I could take back.

Rodney was out of town taking care of some business and I had just come home from having a girl's night out with my friends. I really wasn't a party girl, but they talked me into going, plus being in that house and day and night without Rodney was making me lonely.

I ran to the bathroom to use it when I walked through the door. I had just finished washing my hands when I heard the front door shut. I knew it was Bishop because he was the only one that had a key to our house. I staggered into the living room, barely able to walk. Bishop was wobbling and I could tell that he was fucked up too.

"Shit, what you doing here Nae Nae?" he slurred.

"Huh? I live here." I shook my head as I flopped down on the couch.

"Shit, you do don't you? Damn." He had a stupid grin on his face.

I stared at him and it was crazy how much he and his brother looked alike. They both were caramel with light brown eyes and smiles that any woman would fall for. If you didn't know any better, you would think that they were twins.

The next thing I knew, I felt a hand on my thigh. The liquor already had me horny and the fact that he looked just like my baby had me really messed up. He pressed his lips against mine and shoved his tongue down my throat. I could taste the liquor with a mix of weed, but I still returned the kiss. I knew what I was doing is wrong but I did just like Jamie Foxx said to do and blamed it on the liquor. He pushed me back and laid me down on the couch while climbing on top of me.

"We can't Bishop. What about Rodney?" I asked.

"Shhh, I won't tell if you don't," he slurred.

Before I could protest anymore, I felt his hardness slide into my warmth.

"Uhh," I moaned.

"See, I knew you wanted it just as bad I as I do. I don't know why you be playing," he said as he pumped away.

The whole night I made love to my boyfriend's older brother. To make matters worse, Rodney came home three days later and I made love to him like nothing ever happened. A month later, I found out I was pregnant. Rodney went to his grave never knowing what happened between me and his brother.

"Yo baby!" Micah said, walking into the room and shaking me from my thoughts.

"Yea," I said, turning around to face him.

"What's wrong? You didn't hear me calling you?" he asked.

"No, I'm sorry. What's up?" I walked over to him giving him a kiss.

"My lil mama said you was running from the boogie man, so I came to see what was up," he said eyeing me.

"Oh, we were just playing a game. Nothing you need to worry about," I said, putting on a fake smile.

"Alright, well come on downstairs so I can cook. You look like you need a break. Daddy got you." He smiled.

"I appreciate it," I said genuinely.

Chapter 3

Reneice

I was so tired of being in this hellhole, so much that it was driving me crazy. I wanted to know what was that bullshit that lawyer was popping about requesting a speedy trial. Seemed to me her ass was a damn speedy lie! I had been in here almost a damn month and had yet to go to trial. I was stressed out, my blood pressure was sky high and to top it all off, I had found out that I was pregnant, yet again. *This shit is crazy.*

I had been avoiding everybody. I denied all visits unless they were from my lawyer. I really wasn't in the mood to see anybody, simply because I didn't have anything to say to anybody. The only people I did call and talk to were Pop-Pop, my daddy, and Mykell.

I was sitting in my cell getting my hair braided by my cell mate Big Mama. She's in here sitting on a murder charge also for killing a man who tried to rape her daughter. I can't say that I blamed her because I would do the same thing if anybody dare tried to touch Amyricale. Just thinking about my kids made me sick, I missed them so much. It broke my heart when MJ told me that Amyricale thought I left because I didn't love her anymore.

"Have you told you're husband about the baby yet?" Big Mama asked.

"No, not yet," I sighed.

"Well why not? I think you should tell him," she said.

"I will, eventually."

"Jones, you have a lawyer visit," one of the guards said just as Big Mama was finishing the last braid.

I was led to the room where I saw Toni's little stuck up ass sitting there.

"Hello Reneice, how are you?"

"Fine, I guess."

"So I'm going to get right to the chase, the witness has suddenly gone missing but the DA still wants to go through with the charges. The trial will start Monday at 9:00 am sharp. This case could actually work in your favor with the witness not wanting to participate."

"So I'll be able to go home?" I asked.

"Hopefully, it's pretty much the witness' word against yours right now. Besides they might not have enough evidence and you'll just plead self-defense."

"Alright, that's fine."

"So I'll call your husband and give him the details."

I went back to my cell with a little hope. As soon as I got back, Big Mama was on me with the questions. I told her everything Toni said and she was genuinely happy for me. I don't really click with females but I really took a liking to Big Mama.

"Oh, I almost forgot. You got some mail," she said, handing me an envelope.

I was shocked to see Kamil's name on it. I haven't spoken to him since the day I got married. I opened it up and was not prepared for what I was about to read.

Dear Neicey,

I know I've apologized thousands of times for leading you on and deceiving you but I really want you to know that I honestly do love you. Whenever I told you that, I never lied. I meant it every time. I was informed that you were in jail and it broke my heart. What really hurt me was the fact that you're there because of me. I know you're probably trying to figure out what I mean so I'm going to come right out and tell you. I'm the key witness in your case. I truly am sorry because you are not supposed to be the one sitting in a cell right now, your so called husband is. The only reason I'm not willing to testify is because of the love I have for you.

Every day I sit back and think about how perfect we were for each other. I will never understand why you chose someone who doesn't appreciate you over me. I mean look at everything you've been through because of him. Is that really what you want? You probably feel obligated to him which is the only reason why you decided to marry him, but it's cool. I know you still love me too. I can tell by the way you kept me around. When you and that nigga don't work out, I'll be there to pick up the pieces; like always,

I love you,

Kamil.

I read that letter like ten times thinking I read the wrong thing. Did he really turn snitch because he was feeling salty? Who does shit like that? I think for the first time in all my years of being on this earth, I was actually speechless; utterly speechless.

I never would have thought he would do something like this. This topped him working with his hoe ass cousin to take me out the game. I was honestly hurt right then. How do you write some shit like this and then have the audacity to put I love you at the end of it?

Mykell

I pulled up to the address the realtor gave me. I looked at the house and instantly knew this was the one for us. When Neicey came home, I wanted us to have a fresh start. I wanted to have a house built from the ground up, but I was a little pressed for time. I wanted everything already moved in by time she got home, I brought MJ along with me to get his opinion.

I looked behind to see MJ pulling up behind me. I just shook my head; you can't tell that little nigga nothing ever since I bought him a car. I told him to tag along so I could get his opinion. He knew his mother's taste and what she would like just as much as I did.

"I'm feeling this one, pops," MJ said, walking over to me as I got out the car.

"Me too, I think this might be the one," I agreed.

I looked at my vibrating phone to see Toni's name on the caller I.D. I just hit the ignore button and sent her to voicemail. I don't know what it is about her ass but she just doesn't seem to understand that no means no. No matter how many times I decline, she still insists on throwing the pussy at me. If she would have met my ass a couple of years earlier when I was a dog, I would have hopped on that shit. But I'm a married man now and I only have eyes for my wife. Her ass better get with it.

"Hello, Mr. Jones," Mr. Parker, my realtor, said as MJ and I approached him.

"What's the details?" I asked

"The house has eight bedrooms including a master bedroom with five bathrooms, a finished basement with a theater room, high ceilings; it also comes with a pool. The kitchen has all stainless steel appliances, with marble countertops; the counters in the bathrooms are also marble."

As MJ and I examined the house, I was sold. This house had Neicey written all over it. I knew she would love.

"This is the one, pops," said MJ, confirming my thoughts.

"We'll take it," I said to Mr. Parker.

After doing all the paperwork, I was handed the keys. I was content with my decision. I walked MJ to his car as we prepared to leave.

"Where you headed to?" I asked.

"I got a little shorty I'm meeting up with." He smiled.

"Alright, lil nigga. Don't be trynna make me a grandpa anytime soon," I laughed.

"Never that, I stay strapped. I don't want ma killing my ass. I'll leave all that baby making to y'all."

"Good, when she get home, we just might make another one," I half joked.

"Alright now old man," MJ laughed before backing up.

As I walked back to my car, Toni called me again. *Fuck it,* I thought as I answered.

"Yo," I said into the phone.

"I really don't like being ignored Mykell."

"What do you want Toni?" I said, ignoring her.

"I need you to meet up with me. I have something very important you might like to hear."

"Don't bullshit me Toni. I don't have time to play with you."

“I’m too grown for games. Just bring ya ass, I’ll text you the address,” she said as she hung up.

I just shook my head at her crazy ass. *Lord give me the strength.*

It seems like Toni’s crazy ass doesn't know how to take a damn hint. I don’t know how many times I have to tell her ass I don’t want her. The hell I look like fucking another bitch while my wife is locked up, possibly facing a double murder charge? The same exact bitch that was supposed to be defending her. I may have done some shit in the past but that shit is dead. I put all that behind me the day I said ‘I do’.

I walked into the restaurant in search of this crazy bitch. It was time I set her ass straight.

“I’m happy you came, I don’t know why you be playing. I know you want me just as bad as I want you,” she said standing up.

"Come here," I said, pulling her close to me so I could whisper in her ear. "Let me tell you something. If it's that easy for me to get it, I don't want it. You barely know me but you ready to drop them panties. My girl made a nigga work hard for it and I damn near chased her ass, which is exactly why I made her my wife," I said before walking away, leaving her looking dumb.

“I wouldn’t play with me if I was you, Mykell. Maybe you forgot that I’m still your wife’s lawyer. Her trial starts in a couple of days and even though it’s looking good for her right now, it would be a shame if something just so happens and she never came home again.”

I turned around and charged her ass grabbing her by her neck, not giving a damn about us being in public. "I don't take being threatened very well, especially when it comes to my wife. Let her ass not come home and I swear your last fucking breath will be a painful one. Play with me if you want to bitch," I said, squeezing tighter before finally letting go.

"Whatever, just make sure you have your ass in court Monday at 9:00," she yelled.

I walked out without looking back. I would never let any bitch or nigga disrespect Neicey; I don't care how mad we get at each other. If Neicey didn't have to go to court in a couple of days, I would have just offed that bitch today.

Lani

Whoever said that 'everything that glitters ain't gold' never lied. I was basically living a lie and hiding from my family. The shit I was going through now, I never had to worry about when I was with Ramone. I haven't spoken to my dad in weeks and that's not like me. *Damn I miss him.*

"Lani, bring yo ass down here!" Zamier yelled.

I just rolled my eyes and headed towards the stairs. His ass gets on my nerves so bad, it don't make no sense.

"What?"

"Who the fuck you think you talking to? You better watch that damn attitude before I put my foot up yo ass," he yelled.

"First of all, you need to stop all that damn yelling. My daughters are upstairs sleep. Wake em up if you want to and we..."

I didn't even get to finish what I was saying before I felt a blow to my face. I stood there in shock for a second before I came back to myself. I charged him like a damn raging bull.

"Don't you ever put yo muthafucking hands on me, bitch," I said as I was trying to hit him, but he was too big and powerful.

He knocked me on my ass and kicked me in my ribs. I doubled over in pain. "Since you wanna be childish and act like a child, Imma treat yo ass like one," he yelled.

All of a sudden, my skin started stinging from the leather belt he was hitting me with. "STOP!" I yelled, but it fell on deaf ears.

"Mommy!" I heard Ranyla yelling from the stairs. I looked up to see her crying.

"When I get back, I want you and your daughters out of my shit. Go back to that nigga that don't want yo ass," he said before walking towards the stairs.

Ranyla ran down to me as I slowly tried to get off the floor. A sharp pain hit me in my ribs and I wanted to scream but I didn't want to scare NyNy any more than she already was.

Enough was enough. I should have left his ass when he came home drunk one night talking about how he paid the doctors at the hospital to fuck up the DNA test on Zyla to make it say he was the father.

I slowly walked up the stairs with NyNy sniffling behind me. "Princess, I need you to be a big girl and do mommy a favor okay? Can you do mommy a favor?" I asked.

She nodded her head up and down. "Yes, mommy."

"Okay, I need you to grab your sister's bag and put whatever you can fit in there. Anything of hers and yours okay?"

She ran out the room and I grabbed my phone to call my brother.

"Yo!" Mykell answered on the second ring.

"Kell, I need you. I need you now."

"What's wrong baby girl?" he asked.

"I'm on my way to you."

"I'll be ready for you."

Four hours later, my daughters and I landed at Miami International Airport. I spotted Mykell's Navigator by the entrance. I wanted to run to him so bad, but the pain in my side prevented me from doing that.

“You don’t have any bags?” he asked jumping out.

“I only packed for the girls,” I said, slowly climbing into the truck.

“What’s wrong? Why you moving like that?”

“Mommy…” Ranyla started but I cut her off.

“Not now NyNy,” I said. “We’ll talk later,” I said turning to Mykell.

He just nodded his head.

We pulled up to a nice house that I’ve never seen before and my mouth hit the floor. “Who lives here?” I asked.

“I do, Imma surprise Neicey with it when she comes home.” He smiled. “Oh, by the way, her trial starts Monday. So you came right on time.”

“You are so sweet.” I smiled.

“I get that a lot,” he joked.

We walked into the house and I was in awe. It was so beautiful.

“Close ya mouth before a bug fly in it,” Mykell laughed.

“Shut up.”

“NyNy, Amyricale is upstairs,” he said. The moment those words left his mouth, she took off running up the stairs. He walked over to me and took Zyla out my arms while grabbing my face. “Start talking, now.”

I slowly sat on the couch before speaking. "If I tell you, you gotta promise that you won't tell daddy," I said in a childlike tone. Even though Kell is the hotter tempered one, I always told him stuff before I did Micah or my daddy.

"It all depends on what you're about to tell me," he said, staring at me while bouncing his niece on his lap.

I wasn't worried though because he never told on me when I asked him not to.

I sighed. "Zamier hit me…"

"WHAT!" he roared. "So you're sitting up here telling me that a nigga put his hands on *my* sister but you don't want me to say nothing? That's cool, I'll let my bullets do all the talking for me."

Zyla looked at her uncle and started giggling like she understood what he was saying.

"See, even my niece agrees."

"That's not all," I said.

"What else?"

"He told me that he paid the doctors to mess up the DNA test when Zyla was born. He also got mad and beat me with a belt after kicking me in my ribs."

He got up and put Zyla on the couch and started pacing the floor. I watched him pace a good five minutes before he spoke again.

"So that's why yo as was crying on the phone? And you think I'm not about to tell Pops that a nigga was beating on his daughter? His *only* daughter. Fuck that

Le'Lani, I don't care what you talking about, I'm telling him," he said as he took his phone out of his pocket.

I got nervous and jumped up, pain shot through my side but I didn't care at that moment. "Kell, please don't. Not yet at least, wait until after the trial. He's already stressing over Neicey; I don't need him stressing over me right now," I pleaded.

He sighed. "Alright. You need to go to the doctors or something?"

"No I'm just going to take a hot bath and soak," I said.

"Alright, pick whatever room you want that don't got kid shit in it and get comfortable because you won't be going back anytime soon," he said, and I knew better than to argue. I just walked up to him and kissed him on the cheek. I was grateful that I have such an understanding brother.

Kamil

Hiding out does not work for a nigga like me. I got the damn police on my ass, mad because I didn't want to testify, they were trying to threaten me but I really didn't give a fuck. That's the last thing I was worried about right then. What I was trying to figure out is why Neicey would do some bullshit like turning herself in for that nigga. I just knew for damn sure that my plan would work, but I guess not.

The plan was to get Mykell locked up. I already knew that nigga had two strikes on him; three strikes and you're out. When he got locked up I was going to get in where I fit it with Neicey and we were supposed to be happy. Unfortunately, she threw a wrench in my plans and fucked everything up.

See, she's supposed to be wearing my ring; not that nigga's. After all the bullshit she's been through because of him, she was still quick to marry his ass. I wasn't tripping though because I knew it would only be a matter of time before he fucks up again. A little birdie told me that Neicey's lawyer wanted Mykell, so all he had to do is fuck up this one time and she'd come home to daddy. All that's left to do is play the waiting game.

Chapter 4

Reneice

This was it. Today was the day. Hopefully everything worked out in my favor because I couldn't imagine spending any more time behind bars. I just hoped Kamil kept his word and stayed far away today. I woke up early as hell today because I couldn't sleep.

"Jones, come with me," the guard said.

I followed him to the room where Toni was waiting for me. She put some clothes on the table. "Your husband brought these for you to put on," she said.

It seemed like she had an attitude but I really don't give a damn about her uppity ass right then. The only thing on my mind was my freedom.

I took the braids out so my hair had a curly look to it. Just because I was in jail didn't mean that I had to look like it. The least I could do was look presentable in front of the judge. When I got in the courtroom, I was happy to see my family. Pop-Pop, my daddy, Micah, Janae, Mykell, MJ, Ramone and Lani; even Jason, Howie, and Corey came down.

"All rise!" the bailiff said and everyone stood to their feet while he judge entered. I was surprised to see that the judge was a woman; a black woman at that. The judge started talking and asking questions but I tuned her out to say a quick prayer.

Lord, you and I both know that I did not commit this crime so I ask that you get me through this. Amen.

I was shaken from my thoughts when the judge asked for the prosecutor to bring forth their witness.

"Um, Your Honor, it seems that our witness has disappeared," said the DA, whose name is Carter.

"Your witness as disappeared huh?" she asked sarcastically.

"Your Honor, I would like to request a quick sidebar," Toni said.

The judge agreed and they walked up to the judge. I don't know what they were saying and I was kind of getting nervous. Toni walked back to me and smiled. I wanted to return the smile but I was too scared to.

"Mr. Carter, since you have no witness and no evidence, I'm giving you a week to come up with some evidence or I'm dismissing this case," she said before banging her gravel. I let out a sigh of relief at those words. I wanted to get up and jump for joy but I didn't want to jump to conclusions.

Three days later

"Neicey, where did you get all this pretty hair from?" Big Mama asked.

"My mama had some pretty hair, so I guess it's genetics. My daddy got a good grade, too."

"You sure one of them wasn't mixed with nothing?"

"Honestly, I don't really know. My mom's family didn't want anything to do with her when she started messing with my daddy. They damn near lost their minds when they found out she was pregnant with my brother, so we never got to meet them. As far as my dad, we never met his side of the family and he never talks about them," I sighed.

"That's deep. I understand the feeling though. Well, I sure do hope this baby comes out with some pretty hair. I have a feeling that it's going to be a girl and Big Mama hasn't been wrong on guessing the sex of a baby yet," she smiled.

"Oh Lord, another one of me running around? I don't know if I can handle that, Amyricale is already a hot mess." I laughed.

"So I'm guessing you still haven't told him," she said, eyeing me.

"Not yet Big Mama, but I promise I will very soon," I said.

"Alright child, it's your business."

"Jones, pack up. You're going home," a guard said.

"Huh? What you say?" I asked confused.

"You're going home, girl. C'mon unless you want to stay here," the guard laughed.

"Hell no!" I yelled. "I don't need anything. Big Mama can keep it all," I said before turning to her and hugging her.

"You have my number, so make sure you keep in touch," I said before leaving.

"Hello Mrs. Jones," Toni greeted me.

"Toni, what happened? I thought the judge gave the DA a week?"

"Yea, but he had a change of heart and decided to drop the charges for the lack of evidence with no witness. Congratulations, you are a free woman," she smiled.

"Oh my God, please tell me you're not playing with me," I said

"I kid you not. Your ride is outside."

After changing my clothes and collecting everything they took from me the first day I got here, I ran outside and was confused when I saw Lakey instead of Mykell; but I was still happy.

"Lakeyyyy!" I yelled.

"Wassup Snook, how does it feel to be free again?" he laughed.

"Shut up," I laughed with him.

We jumped in his truck and pulled out of the driveway. The whole ride we talked about everything. He informed me that Mykell had bought MJ a car and I didn't know how I felt about that; but there was really nothing I could do about it.

We pulled up to Lakey's house and he killed the engine. "I got you some clothes and shit for you to take a shower. We got one more stop to make before I drop you off at home," he said.

* * *

After a nice, long, hot shower, I felt rejuvenated. We drove for quite a while before Lakey pulled up to this beautiful house. Whoever lived here was lucky. If I lived here, I would never leave the house. He sent a quick text before he hopped out of the car and told me to do the same.

"Who lives here Lakey?" I asked as he unlocked the door.

"My homey," was all he said.

"Well your homey has it going on, this house is the shit," I said in admiration.

I followed him into the dining room. And stopped dead in my tracks.

"SURPRISE! WELCOME HOME!" everyone yelled.

Tears instantly started to fall from my eyes. My eyes met with Mykell's and no words needed to be said. I took off running and jumped into his arms. I kissed him passionately and let him know that whatever was said before was forgiven and I didn't care at that point.

"I missed you so much," I said after we finally broke the kiss.

"I missed you more," he said.

"Umm is he the only one yo ass see? Damn," Ramone said.

"Shut up, nigga," I laughed.

"Welcome home, Ladybug," he said as we hugged.

"Y'all acting like her ass just did fifteen years or something," Micah joked.

"Don't go there Mack Daddy, you know you missed me," I laughed.

"MOMMY!" Romell, Tyriq and Amyricale yelled while running towards me.

"Hey babies, I missed y'all so much," I cried while kissing them all over their faces.

"Don't be a bad girl no more, mommy, okay?" Amyricale said.

"Alright, I won't."

"Where's your brother?" I asked.

"You know I'm not too far behind," MJ said, walking into the room.

"Hey handsome." I smiled hugging my oldest son. That boy is his father's son.

"Snook, I want you to meet somebody," Lakey said, walking my way followed by a pretty female. "Snook, this is Daniella, Daniella this is Neicey."

"Nice to finally meet you; you can call me LaLa. I've heard a lot about you," she smiled.

"Don't listen to anything he told you about me, I'm not that bad," I laughed.

"Yea, right," Lakey huffed and everyone laughed.

I looked around, seriously happy to be home. Even though I was only gone for a little over a month, it felt I was away from my family forever.

Micah

Janae must have thought that I'm some type of dumb nigga or something. Her phone stayed ringing at all times or the day and night but she acted like she didn't wanna answer when I'm around. My daughter and son already told me that some nigga came by the house to see her, and ever since that day she has been acting all types of funny.

See, all that showing out and confrontation shit ain't my style. I just sat back and waited for her to tell me what's up, or wait for the shit to blow up. Either way, I chose to remain cool. Everybody's having a good ass time and just sitting around laughing and Jana's phone is ringing for what seems to be the hundredth time since we'd been here.

"I'll be right back," she said like she was irritated.

I looked over at Kell and he must have known something was up. We sent each other a silent message and he looked over at Mone and got his attention and nodded his head towards the basement door. That's the type of relationship I had with lil bro, we could communicate without even opening our mouths.

As we headed towards the basement, Neicey stopped us dead in our tracks. "Where the hell y'all going?" she asked.

"Nowhere nosey ass," I teased.

"Yea alright, let me find out," she said with her eyebrow raised as she looked at Mykell.

"Ain't nothing. I'm just showing them the setup I got going on in the basement," Mykell said.

She just nodded her head and we took that as our cue to proceed. When we got to the basement, Kell led us to what looked like an office down there. As soon as we were behind closed doors, I spoke what was on my mind.

"Man, what the hell wrong with the females in this family?" I asked as I sat on the couch.

"Shit, not you too?" Mykell shook his head. "I just knew you and Janae would be the ones to not have problems."

"Shit, I think she got some funny shit going on," I said.

"How you figure?" Ramone asked.

"A couple of weeks back, Ranee told me that some man came by to see her mommy and ever since then, she been acting real funny. Somebody be calling her phone all damn day and night and she don't never answer it in front of me. She'll either let it ring or leave out the room to answer it; then she'll talk low so I can't hear what she saying."

"Damn," they both said simultaneously.

"So you think she cheating?" Mone asked.

"I can't call it man." I shook my head.

"I say the next time her phone ring in the middle of the night, yo ass answer it and see who it is," Mykell said.

"I'm with Kell on this one. You'll never know unless you find out for yourself."

I shook my head. "I don't know why I'm even talking to y'all niggas. Y'all have more relationship problems than anybody I know." I laughed.

"This is true," Mykell laughed. "But I'm the only one in this room that's married so shut up," he said, throwing a pen at me.

"I'm surprised. You and Ladybug fight like damn cats and dogs," Mone laughed.

"Don't they? I give it a week before she ready to take his damn head off again," I agreed.

"What the fuck ever. See, what y'all don't know is Neicey ass love that fighting shit because she know at the end of the night I'm not gone argue with her ass, Imma just blow her fuckin back out and tell her to shut the fuck up." Mykell smirked.

"C'mon man. That's still my baby sister. I don't want to hear that shit," Ramone said with his face turned up.

"Whatever dude. You're just saying that because you're not fucking our baby sister no more. She done kicked yo ass to the curb nigga," I laughed.

"What the hell ever! Every time she kiss that nigga, he tasting my dick. I could have Lani whenever I want, but I chose to fall back and let her do her. Besides, I got me somebody I been kicking it with lately anyways."

"Shit between her and that nigga Zamier is done and over with. But how does this 'somebody' feel about you being down here in Florida with the mother of your child?" Mykell asked.

"I'm not with her, I came by myself."

"Nigga please," I said.

"I'm serious, she actually wants me to send for her. She's really set on meeting Neicey."

"Who wanna meet me?" Neicey said, walking through the door scaring the shit out of us.

"When you enter the men headquarters, you knock. The hell wrong with you girl?" I joked.

She playfully rolled her eyes. "Anyways, what y'all talking about? Who wanna meet Neicey?" she asked, walking over to Mykell and sitting on his lap.

"A friend of mines," Ramone said.

"Negative." She shook her head. "I don't like her."

"How you don't like her and don't even know her?" he asked, mushing her head.

"Ain't no bitches allowed in my house unless their names are Le'Lani, Janae and now Daniella; so whoever the trick is, tell her the queen of the castle said no."

"You just don't want to meet her because of Lani; that shit ain't cool, Ladybug."

"My loyalty lies with Lani, not a rebound bitch," she said rolling her neck and I just shook my head. Her ass was a damn firecracker, always ready to go off.

"No, your loyalty is with me, your brother," Ramone said.

"Whatever, anyways I just came down to say that me and the girls are taking the kids out for a little while so y'all can sit here and talk about nothing until we get back. Daddy and Pop-Pop are going somewhere too," she said, getting up.

"You going dressed like that?" I asked, looking at her short shorts and tank top.

"Bye Micah!" she yelled walking out the door.

"I love that girl," I laughed.

"Then you can take her ass home with you," Mykell said shaking his head.

Mykell

Thank God I had my phone on silent, all day Toni's crazy ass had been blowing up my damn phone. My wife wasn't locked up anymore, so therefore she had no reason to contact me anymore. I think she has a damn death wish or something, if Neicey finds out, it's a rap for her ass. *Hell, she might just kill my ass too.* I shook my head as I read a text message I received two minutes.

Toni: I don't know how many times I have to tell you, I don't like being ignored. I don't give a damn if wifey is home. Call me back!

"Yo, this bitch is nuts!" I said.

"What bitch?" Micah asked.

"Toni," I sighed.

"Who the fuck is Toni?"

"Neicey's lawyer."

Ramone whistled. "I know damn well you did not fuck her lawyer, Kell."

"Shit, the way she sweating a nigga, I might as well have. She don't understand what the fuck no means. She better be glad I don't want Neicey thinking we had something going on or I would unleash her on that ass."

Ramone got up and walked over to the bar. "I think you need a drink because you ass in some deep shit," he laughed. "What kind words would you like me to say at your funeral? No doubt about it, Ladybug is definitely going to kill yo ass."

"Man, I ain't even fucked the bitch," I huffed.

"C'mon Kell, you know that's going to be hard to tell her when the bitch acting like you already laid the pipe down. You know the women in this family is crazy as hell and they stick together; so that means we all in some shit when Neicey find out," Micah laughed.

"Shit, we just might have to find another lawyer because she's going to kill both of y'all." Mone shook his head.

Before I could even respond, I saw my phone lighting up again. *This bitch is cuckoo for cocoa puffs.*

"What Toni!"

"Is that really how you answer your phone?" she chuckled.

"Why the fuck are you calling me? My wife is home now, so your services are no longer needed."

"See, now, that's where you're wrong. I did you a favor so you owe me one and I'm pretty sure you already know what I want, so don't fucking play with me."

I didn't even finish listening to what her crazy ass had to say before I hung up. All eyes were on me when I got off the phone and the only thing I could do was shrug.

"Either you get rid of her ass or Neicey will do it for you," Micah said.

"Forget all that, we have more important issues to discuss," I said.

"Like what?" Mone asked.

"Like why all of a sudden the police sniffing around some murders that happened, what, two years ago? The only people that knew about the shit is the family and I know y'all ain't open y'all mouths, so that only leaves one person," I said.

"Kamil," they said at the same time.

"I'm happy to know were all on the same page," I smirked.

"Yea, but why would he wait two years to snitch? That shit doesn't make sense."

"Ain't no telling what be going through that nigga head," I said.

"We should have put a bullet in his head a long damn time ago. I never did like the nigga but he could do no wrong in Ladybug's eyes."

By no means am I an insecure nigga but sometimes I wonder why the hell Neicey did choose to keep this nigga around when she knew he was on some shady shit. That just doesn't sit right with me.

"Yo, do y'all think that Neicey still has feelings for that nigga?" I asked, voicing my thoughts.

They just got quiet and looked away like they didn't hear shit I said.

"Damn, for real?"

"I mean think about it Kell, if you didn't have feelings for somebody would you keep them around?" Micah asked.

I didn't answer; instead I turned to the person who knew her better than anybody. "How about you Mone, that's your sister and you raised her so you know."

"Shit as much as I hate to admit it, yes she does. Ladybug may have some type of feelings for him but you don't have to worry about shit."

"What you mean?" I asked.

"Check this out, her and Lakey were fucking inseparable when they were little. They had feelings for each other but she left before they could even do anything. Now that they're older they're still close as hell, she made him the damn godfather to y'all kids, but do you feel threatened by him? Do you think they got something going?"

I had to think about it for a minute, he was right. Shit, Lakey been around her all her life and was still around but I never got the feeling that they had anything going on. "Naw," I answered.

"Okay then."

"But that's different though Mone, you gotta think about it differently. Whenever her and Kell had problems, he was there to be a shoulder to cry on, when they broke up, who did she run to? Who was she in a relationship with? When she left to run down here, who did she call? She keeping that nigga close for a reason and what that reason is, we don't know," Micah said.

I just sat back and thought about everything my brother just said. He was right also; she was keeping this nigga close for a reason. Too bad he won't be around too much longer.

MJ

My main thing, Chyanne, called me and said she had something really important to talk to me about. I didn't want to leave my mom but her and my aunties were going somewhere anyway, so it worked out perfectly fine. I pulled up to her house to see her waiting for me on the porch. I got out and walked up to her. She didn't look right and I could tell that she had been crying.

"What's wrong baby?" I asked.

She mumbled something but I didn't understand what she said because her head was down. I kneeled down in front of her and lifted her head up. "Look at me, now what's wrong."

"I'm pregnant," she cried.

Whoa, "Okay…um." I didn't know what to say.

"He touched me," she said in a low whisper.

"Wait, what? Who?" I asked.

"My daddy….he touched me and my mom don't believe me." She broke down.

I was shocked. The only thing I could do was pull her into my arms and let her cry. All of a sudden the door opened and her dad walked out, he smelled like he took a damn dive in a swimming pool of liquor. Instantly my blood began to boil.

"What the fuck I tell you? I told yo ass to stay in yo fucking room!" he yelled, grabbing Chyanne by her hair.

"AHHHH!" she screamed, pleading with her eyes for me to save her.

I don't know what came over me but I punched him dead in his shit. He stumbled back while putting his hand up to his bleeding nose. "Chy go get in the car, now!" I said, never taking my eyes off of her bitch ass daddy. She ran down the stairs to my car.

"You little muthafucka!" he yelled while charging at me. He swing and hit me in the eye but that didn't do anything but piss me off more. Before I knew it, I lost my damn mind on his ass. If it wasn't for Chyanne's screaming, I probably would have killed his ass. I looked down at his bloody face and ran down the steps.

"Are you okay?" she asked.

"Forget about me, are you okay?" I asked.

She just nodded her head. I grabbed my phone and dialed the first person that popped in my head.

"Hello?"

"Ma, I need you."

Fifteen minutes later, we were pulling up to my house. I couldn't even get out the car before my mom came running out the house. She ran right up to my side of the car.

"What's wrong MJ?" she asked. When she saw my face and knuckles, she damn near lost her mind. "Lani, go grab my boyfriend. Shit just got fucking real!" she yelled at my auntie, referring to her gun.

"Ma, chill. You just got home and don't need to be going back," I chuckled.

That's what I loved about my mom; she asked no questions and was always ready to go to war. I got out of the car and went to open the door for Chyanne. We all walked into the house with all eyes on us.

"Umm, ma and pops, I need to talk to y'all," I said before grabbing Chyanne's hand, leading the way to the kitchen.

"What the fuck happened to you face?" my dad roared, walking over to me and examining my face.

"I got into a fight with her old man," I said.

"What happened MJ?" my mom asked.

"I went over there to talk to Chyanne and she told me that..." I stopped and looked over at her. "I think I'll let her tell you."

She looked at me like she was scared. "It's okay, you can talk to them," I reassured her.

"Um...my dad he...he likes to touch me and I'm...I'm pregnant." She shifted uncomfortably.

"Damn," my pops said.

My mom looked like she was about to have a heart attack. "I know it might sound harsh, but I just want to know. Are you pregnant by MJ or your dad?" she asked.

"I...I don't know." She broke down crying. My mom rushed up to her and hugged her.

“I got her, you two finish,” she said, walking out of the kitchen with Chyanne.

I looked up at my dad and could tell he had a mouthful to say. “MJ, did we not just have this discussion about you strapping up? How old is she? Do I need to go beat this nigga ass?” he said all in one breath.

I sighed before I answered. “Honestly pops, I don’t know how this shit happened. We used a condom every time, but one time it broke and I never thought anything of it. She’s sixteen and I never knew what the hell was going on with her dad. I went over there to talk to her, then all of a sudden he started acting crazy. I just flipped on him; he caught me one good time in my eye. His drunk ass probably won’t even remember what happened.”

I watched as my pops paced back and forth in the kitchen. I knew his mind was running because mine was too. *Me, a dad?*

“A baby though, MJ?” he asked.

“It wasn’t planned.”

“I know but…damn.”

We both looked up when we heard my mom come back into the kitchen. Ma was a loose cannon, so we didn’t know what to expect, especially me.

“I gave her some painkillers and let her take a nap. She wants to talk when she wakes up,” she said.

“Come here, ma,” I said.

She went to the freezer and got some ice and put it in a sandwich bag before coming to me. She turned my face then put the ice on my left eye. She looked at me with sad eyes.

“Look ma, I never meant for all this to happen. I’ll be sixteen in a couple of weeks and I know that’s not any better, but I’m man enough to take care of my responsibilities. If that is my baby, I’ll take care of it…even if it’s not mines,” I said.

She didn’t say anything; she just looked at me hard before walking back into the living room with everyone else.

“You know yo mom is a little emotional, don’t sweat it. She heard you loud and clear and she understands,” my pops said before leaving out behind her.

What Imma do now?

Chapter 5

Janae

We had been home for a week and things between me and Micah had been real intense. When he looked at me, I didn't see the love in his eyes anymore. I felt like I was slowly losing him, but that's not what I wanted to happen. I really wanted to tell him about Bishop, but I just didn't know how.

"WHAT BISHOP!" I yelled into the phone.

"Janae, do you take me as a fucking joke or something?"

"Stop calling my phone Bishop. I'm not playing with you."

"Janae just take the damn test!"

I just hung up the phone, frustrated. This shit is getting ridiculous. *I wish Micah would hurry up and get home,* I thought. I heard the doorbell ring, so I ran down the stairs. I wish I would have looked out the peephole before I opened the damn door.

"Why the hell are you at my house?"

"Because you like to play me as a damn fool."

"Bishop, leave. Me. The. Fuck. Alone," I said.

He brushed past me and walked into the house and I damn near fainted. Bishop never put his hands on me or anything but I didn't like being around him when I was by myself. The last time we were by ourselves, we did the unthinkable.

"This is nice," he said, eyeing my house. "You know, I'm starting to think you like the fucking attention, because all you have to do is take the test then I will get the fuck on."

"She's not your daughter Bishop, what part of that do you not understand?" I asked with my hands on my hips.

"How do you know? If I'm correct you fucked me then fucked my brother a few days later, then you started hollering you were pregnant. My brother went to his grave thinking that little girl was his and she's probably not."

I sighed in frustration. "I'm sick of this shit," I said walking into the kitchen, and of course his ass just had to follow me. "Bishop I…" I froze when I heard a car pull up. I looked out the window in the kitchen and saw Micah's truck. *Oh shit.*

"Bishop, you gotta go!" I panicked.

"Fuck that, I'm not running," he said.

"Oh my God, I hate you!" I said with venom dripping from my voice.

I heard the front door open so I ran to the living room.

"Mommy guess what?" Ranee said.

"What baby?" I asked.

"Daddy…" she started but stopped.

I turned around to see Bishop standing there. Why the hell couldn't his ass just stay locked up?

"I hope I'm not interrupting," Micah said from behind me.

I wanted to turn around but I couldn't; I was stuck.

"That's rude, Nae Nae, introduce us," Bishop smirked.

"Shut. Up," I said through gritted teeth.

"Baby girl, take your brother upstairs for me," said Micah to Ranee.

Ranee did as she was told and grabbed her brother's hand, slowly walking him up the stairs. I was still facing Bishop, too scared to turn around to face Micah; I didn't want to see the look on his face.

"Turn the fuck around," Micah said. Janae was scared because she had never heard him talk like that in all the years we have been together. She slowly turned around and saw the fire in his eyes.

"Now, you got two minutes to tell me what the fuck is going on in *my* house. Start talking," he said sternly.

"Um...well...Bishop is Rodney's brother and he came to see Ranee," I said, leaving the most important part out.

I watched as his eyes shifted from me to Bishop. "What you got to say playboy?"

"I'm here for a DNA test, Nae Nae knows that," said Bishop as I slowly felt my world caving in.

Micah looked shocked at what Bishop had just revealed and the only thing I could do was close my eyes and say a silent prayer.

"Word, on who?" Micah asked.

"On Ranee. We should have had one done years ago but she was too busy running, trying to avoid the shit. I got tired of chasing her ass."

"Alright," Micah shook his head. "Imma let y'all handle y'all business. I'm out," he said walking towards the door.

"Micah wait!" I said chasing after him.

"You know, I actually thought you were different from all the rest of these dirty bitches out here, maybe I need to reevaluate my decision," he said with venom dripping from his voice.

"Just hear me out, please?" I was damn near begging.

He just hopped in his car and rolled the window down. "Go in the house and take care of that, I'll be back." With that, he pulled out of the driveway.

Feeling defeated, I walked back into the house. "We can go get the test done tomorrow. After we get these results back, I want nothing to do with you. Now get out," I said on the verge of tears.

He just nodded his head and left. I sat on the couch and cried my eyes out; wondering if this would be the end of me and Micah.

Micah

I drove around for a few with this shit weighing heavy on my mind. Like did she seriously just tell me that her deceased ex-boyfriend's brother wanted a DNA test on her daughter? What the hell did I miss?

I called Mykell to tell him about this bullshit.

"Hello?" Neicey answered.

"Mannn, tell me why yo girl ain't shit!" I said, shaking my head.

"What's wrong Mack Daddy?"

"So I walk in the house with the kids to find Janae ass in there with another nigga. Come to find out that's Ranee's uncle."

"Okay…"

“Here’s the kicker though. He’s talking about all he wanted was a damn DNA test on Ranee but Janae kept giving his ass the runaround.

“Wait, so that means…OH SHIT! Kell come here,” she yelled.

“Yo!” Mykell said into the phone.

I told him everything I had just told Neicey, then the phone went quiet for a few seconds.

“Damn! She was fucking brothers, dog!” he finally said.

“Looks that way huh?”

“You know Neicey had to call her ass up, she on the phone with her now.”

“Right now, I really don’t give a fuck. This shit is real crazy because it’s like I was really thinking about putting a ring on her finger and shit. Now I’m thinking about how well do I really know her? What else is she hiding from me? Hell, is Baby Mack mine or yours?”

“Nigga, what? I ain’t fucked her, man,” he said.

I chuckled when I heard Neicey in the background yelling he had better not have. “Man, let me call y’all crazy asses back.”

I drove a little bit more before I decided to go back home because there was some shit that Janae and I needed to talk about. When I pulled up, all the lights were out but I knew that she wasn’t asleep. I went upstairs to check on the kids. They were sleeping peacefully, so I headed to my room.

I took a deep breath before I went in. I heard the shower running so I just sat on the bed and waited for her to come out. While I waited I rolled myself a blunt, knowing I would need it.

"You scared the shit out of me!" Janae said while grabbing her chest.

"My bad," I said as I exhaled the weed. "Did you take care of that?"

"Yea, we have an appointment next week."

I just nodded my head.

"Look Micah, I know what you think and it wasn't like that. Me and Bishop were drunk when it happened and it only happened one time."

"So if you knew it happened, why did you not get the test done as soon as she was born? You let his brother go to the grave thinking Ranee was his daughter. That is some scandalous shit."

She sighed. "I know for a fact that Ranee is not his, she is Rodney's daughter."

"Yea, well, we will know for sure when the test results come back. So tell me what else are you hiding?"

"I'm not hiding nothing," she said like I offended her.

"You sure? Because I don't want shit else popping up later on down the line. I'm already questioning how well I know you."

She looked at me with hurt in her eyes. "I swear I'm not hiding anything."

I looked around and noticed she took her suitcase out the closet. She probably thought I would tell her to get out or something but that's not the case. No matter what she did in the past, she's still the mother of my child; my first born

"Going somewhere?" I asked.

"Umm yea, Neicey told me to come see her."

Aw shit, I thought. I know exactly what's about to go down. "When you leaving?"

"Two days."

"You taking the kids?"

"I was because I didn't know if..."

"Kill that shit. I'm not the type of nigga to run away from shit. I'll keep the kids," I cut her off.

"Thank you."

"You don't have to thank me, those are my kids," I reminded her.

Reneice

I drove to my old condo that I used to live in when I first moved down here. Since Lakey owned it, he agreed to let Chyanne stay here until she figured out what she wanted to do. We tried to call her mother and father multiple times, but not one time did they answer.

I knocked on the door waiting for an answer. “Hey boo,” I said, hugging Chyanne when she answered.

“Hey Mama Neicey. How are you?”

“I’m good, but I came to take you to the doctors. MJ told me you haven’t been to the doctor to see how far along you are so I made you an appointment as well as one for myself.”

“What you need an appointment for?” she asked with a raised eyebrow.

“Because,” I sighed, “I’m pregnant my damn self but I need for you not to tell anybody, especially MJ.”

“Oh my God!” she squealed.

“Child, come on before we be late,” I laughed.

On the way to the doctor, I noticed Chyanne was crying.

“Whoa, what’s with the tears, lil mama?” I asked while handing her some tissue.

"I just feel like I messed up a lot of people's lives, including MJ's."

"What, how you figure that?" I asked, confused.

"Because it's like my family has some type of curse on it. All of the women in my family since my great grandma had their first child before their seventeenth birthday. My mom blames me for never being able to follow her dreams. She said if I was never born, she could have been a well-paid doctor. Then the fact that my father likes to have sex with his only child is beyond me. Now I've brought MJ into my messed up life and his life is messed up too. This could either be his child or my damn dad's and I hate that I have to string him along not knowing," she sobbed.

"Chyanne, listen to me. It's not your fault; none of the shit that is happening to you is your fault. Your mother is just hurting but she's mad at the wrong person, it was her decision to lay down and make you, you didn't ask to be made nor born. Your father is just sick, he needs his ass beat seriously and I wanna do it myself. As far as MJ goes, his life is not ruined. You both knew what could possibly happen when you have sex, so it goes both ways. MJ has already made it clear to us that he will step up and be a man but of course, he's not in it by himself because I'm here for both of y'all, as well as his father."

"So, you're not mad at me?" she asked.

I took my eyes from the road to look at her, "No baby, I'm not mad. You know, I see a lot of myself in you."

"Really?"

"I sure do, I see how determined you are to do something with your life. I know how it feels to be violated but you can't let that get you down, you have to beat the odds."

"I've been out looking for a job. I'm still in school and no matter what I'll try to stick it out for as long as I can," she said.

"Well, Daniella, Lakey's girlfriend, she owns this boutique. She already told me she wants me to come work for her because as you know, I have style," I laughed.

"That you do," she laughed with me.

"So how about we see about her hooking you up with a job also."

"Really Mama Neicey? You would do that for me? I would love that then I could actually pay some rent because I feel bad about living there rent free."

"Lil mama, I already told you, I got you." I smiled.

"MJ is so lucky to have you as a mom, he really is. You are so loving and caring."

"Thanks boo," I said as we pulled up to the doctor's office. "Now let's go check on these babies."

Chyanne went first so she wanted me to come back with her. She was so nervous that her hands were trembling. I grabbed her hand as the doctor checked her out.

"Well Ms. Williams, it seems that you are seventeen weeks."

"How many months is that?" Chyanne asked.

"That would put you at four months."

She gasped. "Oh my God, I've been pregnant for three months and didn't know? Is that bad?"

"No, it's not. Some women don't show symptoms right away. I'm just happy you came to us when you did," the doctor said. "I'll write you a prescription for some prenatal vitamins and I have a pamphlet with lots of information for you."

"Thank you," Chyanne smiled.

"Well Mrs. Jones, since you're already in here, I can go right ahead with you next," she said to me.

"That's fine," I said.

"You want me to leave?" Chyanne asked.

"You can stay."

I was shocked when I found out that I was already five months. Now I knew for sure that I got pregnant before the wedding. What's even more shocking is the fact that I'm not even showing yet. Sooner, rather than later, I will have to tell Mykell. She said I could even find out the sex if I wanted to, but I would wait until Mykell came with me to do all that.

After our appointments, I filled our prescriptions and took Chyanne out to lunch. There was something about this girl that I took a liking too. She felt like she didn't have anybody in the world that she can trust or that loved her and I remember feeling like that once upon a time.

"So, I think we need to go on a shopping spree, on Mykell of course," I said as we ate.

"He has you so spoiled. How long have you guys been together?"

"Nine years, almost ten," I answered.

"I know we're still young, but I hope me and MJ make it that long."

"It wasn't easy boo, trust me on that. I've had my fair share of fighting and heartbreak," I said truthfully.

"I understand. I've been in a few scuffles myself over MJ."

"It something about them damn Jones boys," I chuckled.

"I guess so huh?"

"But you never should be out there fighting over no boy, because at the end of the day, niggas will always be niggas. They will do what they wanna do until they get tired of playing around, and sometimes it takes for them to lose you before they open their eyes."

"I know. It's like MJ wanted to keep us a secret in the beginning. He claimed he didn't like everybody in our business, but the moment he seen me talking to a boy on the basketball team, he threw a fit. After that, he let it be known we were together."

"So how long have you too been kicking it?" I asked.

"About four months now," she smiled.

"Wow," I shook my head.

"Yea, MJ is the first boy I've ever been with…besides my dad," she said with her head down.

I reached across the table and lifted her head up. "You don't have to be ashamed. I'm not judging you."

"Thank you, at least I have someone I can talk to."

"Of course, you can talk to me about anything." I smiled.

My phone starting ringing and, of course, it would be MJ.

"Yea boy?"

"Ma, have you see Chyanne? I went by the house, but she's not answering and her phone keep going to voicemail," he said with concern in his voice.

"She's with me, don't worry. She's in good hands. I took her out for a little girl time, if that's alright with you."

He laughed. "Yea that's cool. Tell her to hit me up when y'all are done."

"I will sweetie."

After we hung up, I delivered the message to Chyanne and she smiled extra hard. I just shook my head at the young couple.

"Alright lil mama, let's go."

"Umm…I was wondering if I could come spend time at your house today."

"Well, c'mon girl, you don't have to ask."

MJ

I was looking for something in my pops' closet for him when I noticed a piece of paper sticking out of a shoe box. Being the lil nosey nigga that I am, I took it out and read it. Apparently Kamil wrote my mom when she was locked up, talking a whole bunch of bullshit about how he's heartbroken because she didn't marry him; so he snitched on my pops.

By time I got done reading the letter, I was boiling. I understand that women become crazy as hell when they're scorned, but did this nigga have to turn into a complete bitch? Especially when he knew what the fuck it was from jump, he knew my pops wasn't going nowhere. Even when I was little and they broke up, my pops was still around, claiming his place. If Kamil was feeling some type of way about my mom getting married, he should have talked to her like a man.

I put the letter in my back pocket and left the room. I texted my Uncle Lakey to let him know I would be stopping by to talk to him about something serious. My dad was throwing a damn fit because Auntie Lani went back to Detroit. I don't know why he's so mad. I mean, she does live there.

He was yelling into the phone when the doorbell rang. I went and opened it.

"Hi Auntie Janae," I said.

"MJ, how are you?"

"I'm good," I said.

I walked over to my pops and let him know I would be back later. The ride to my Uncle Lakey's was a quick one. On the ride there I thought about how I wanted to approach the situation. When I got there, Daniella opened the door. *If only she was a couple of years younger,* I thought as she greeted me.

"He's in his office waiting on you," she said.

"Thank you."

I knocked on the door before going in. "Wassup Unc?"

"You tell me nephew; what's so important?" he asked.

"This," I said handing him the letter. He took his time reading it then looked up at me.

"Yo dad know about this?" he asked.

"Nope, I just so happened to come across it when I was looking for something in their closet. I'm pretty sure she hasn't told anyone about it."

"Thanks for letting me know, I'll handle it."

"Actually Unc, I was planning on handling it myself."

"What you mean?" he asked with a raised eyebrow.

"I think you know what I mean."

He sighed. "Look MJ, I understand, but you know like I know, Neicey will kill both of our asses if I let this go down."

"She don't have to know I did it."

"First of all, what you know about shooting a gun?" he asked.

"Do you know who raised me? Better yet, do you remember who my parents are?"

He just nodded his head. "You mom is gon kill me, but it's your call. I just need you to run yo plan by me before you make any moves. You possibly have a little one on the way, so don't let this shit become a habit."

"Thanks Unc, I just have to find the nigga first," I smiled.

"Yea, you do that. Now get out my house nigga," he laughed.

Chapter 6

Kamil

I felt a little hurt that not one time since Neicey has been home has she tried to reach out to me. I poured my damn heart out in that letter but acting like it didn't mean shit to her. After everything we've been through, she's just going to throw it away for a no good nigga that will sure enough cause her more pain.

All I needed is for that lawyer bitch to step her game up and play her role so Neicey can leave Mykell for good this time and get a divorce. I knew she still loved me but she's too scared to admit it because of him. It's okay because we will have our chance to reunite one day.

I just wanted to hear her voice, that's all I wanted to do. I changed my number, so I knew she'd answer not knowing it's me. The phone rang three times before she answered.

"Hello?"

I smiled when I heard her sweet voice. "Hello?" she said again. Still, I didn't answer her. The line went dead, indicating that she had hung up.

Just hearing her voice stirred up some emotions in me that I knew would never die. All I needed for her to do was open her eyes and realize what's she's missing.

Mykell

Toni's crazy ass had the nerve to text me early this morning talking about she had something very important to talk to me about. Usually, I would have ignored her but I knew that she won't leave me alone until I saw what she wanted. I texted her back and told her I would meet her at her office.

Her secretary walked me back to her office and she was on the phone, so I just sat in the seat until she finished. While she was on the phone, Neicey called me. *Damn.*

"Wassup, Baby?" I answered.

"Why you leave so early? Romell wanted you to sign some paper he said only you could sign," she said.

"My bad, I had some business to take care of. Everybody ready for school? Tyriq didn't give you any problems did he?" I asked.

I noticed Toni had gotten off the phone and she was staring at me. I just ignored her and gave my wife my undivided attention.

"Nope, he was cool. I decided not to send Amyricale to daycare today so I can spend some Mommy and me time with her."

"Alright, I'll see y'all when I get home."

"Okay,"

"Love you."

"Love you more," she said before ending the call.

"How sweet," Toni said sarcastically.

"What do you want? You better not be on no bullshit," I said.

She opened a folder that was lying on her desk and took a picture out. "Do you know him?" she asked.

In my hands was a picture of Kamil, a dead man walking. "Maybe, why?"

"Because he's the reason your wife is not doing life in prison right now. Apparently, he didn't want the woman he loves sitting behind bars; so he refused to cooperate." She smirked.

"Okay, how do you know?" I asked.

"I have my sources. Honestly, I'm not supposed to know this info either, so this stays between us."

"What does this have to do with me?" I asked, not phased with this little info I already knew.

"Maybe your wife is not as faithful as you think if another man is willing not to work with the police so she won't go to prison," she said while walking over to me.

I just shook my head. *This bitch is ditzy.* I got so close to her that our faces were only inches apart. "I don't know how many times I have to tell you, I don't want yo ass. My wife is enough woman for me. Don't fuck with me, I'm not the type of nigga you would like to have as an enemy," I said.

She smiled like she found this shit amusing. "Are you threatening me Mykell?" she chuckled. "I must admit that shit turns me on," she said, grabbing my dick. Shockingly, my shit didn't even get hard. I smacked her ands away and moved back.

"Don't play with me Toni, I'm not gon warn yo ass too many more times," I said before leaving her office.

When I got back to the house, it was quiet thanks to all the kids being in school. Next year, Amyricale would be in school also so that gives me an opportunity to knock Neicey's ass up again. I was standing in the doorway watching Neicey comb Amyricale's hair while Amyricale combed her Barbie's hair.

"Pretty Mommy," Amyricale said.

"Yes baby, you're pretty."

"No mommy, you pretty," Amyricale said, turning around smiling.

"She is pretty huh, MyMy?" I said, finally making my presence known. They both turned their heads in my direction and smiled.

"Daddy!" Amyricale yelled excitedly.

I climbed in the bed and kissed MyMy then kissed Neicey. I noticed when I kissed Neicey she looked at me funny and pulled back faster than she needed to. I walked over to the closet to change into something more comfortable and I could feel her eyes watching. I threw on a wife beater and some basketball shorts. When I came out, Neicey was still eyeing me like she wanted to say something. "What?" I asked.

She didn't say anything but went back to doing Amyricale's hair. I just shook my head and climbed in bed. "Is it alright if I chill with my two favorite girls today?" I asked.

"We're about to leave," Neicey said without looking at me.

"Where y'all going?" I asked.

"Out," she said.

"Okay…" I said waiting for her to elaborate.

"Auntie Nae go eat," Amyricale said, telling me what her mom wouldn't.

"You going out to eat with Auntie Janae?" I asked.

"Yes daddy."

Neicey's phone started ringing and she reached over to grab it. I noticed she was getting a little gut on her. I reached over and poked her stomach and she smacked my hand away. I chuckled while she answered her phone. "Hello?" she said.

She looked at her phone annoyed and rolled her eyes before hanging up.

"Who was that?" I asked.

She just shrugged her shoulders.

"What time y'all leaving?"

"As soon as I finish her hair. I still gotta take my shower."

Five minutes later, Amyricale had pretty ponytails in her hair and was bouncing out the room. I noticed Neicey's attitude had changed and she was acting funny. I went to the door and locked it while she was getting her stuff ready for the shower.

"What's wrong with you?" I asked, walking up behind her.

"Nothing, move." She tried to push me back but I wouldn't move.

"Tell me."

"Where did you go this morning, and don't lie."

"I told you I had to handle some business. Why?" I shrugged.

"Because yo ass walked out of here with the damn room smelling like Irish Spring but you come back smelling like Escada....a woman's perfume," she said, staring me in my eyes like she was daring me to lie.

Shit, "So what you saying?" I said while pulling on the waistband of her shorts.

"I'm not saying shit. I'm waiting for you to do all the talking," she said trying to slap my hand away.

I looked at her like she was crazy. "Are you telling me no?" I asked.

She shoved me away and went to the bathroom. She tried to close the door on me but I was already in. I grabbed her and placed her hands on the counter of the sink.

"Move, Mykell, I'm not thinking about you," she said as I pulled her shorts down and moved her thong to the side, ignoring her the whole time. "Mooove!" she yelled.

I just pulled my dick from my boxers and shorts. I used my leg to spread her legs. I looked up in the mirror to see her glaring at me. I smiled at her mischievously before slamming my already hard dick into her wetness. "Ahhh!" she yelled out.

I pumped faster and faster while grabbing a handful of her hair. The fact that she hated when I pulled her hair fueled me even more. "I hate you," she moaned.

"Shut up." I smacked her ass. "I didn't ask you to speak."

I pulled out, leaving only the tip in and then rammed back inside her; I repeated that a few more times.

"Now, tell me why you're mad. Huh? Why you mad Neicey?" I asked without losing a stroke.

She just moaned without saying anything, she just threw that ass back matching my strokes.

"Oh, now you don't have nothing to say. A few minutes ago you had a lot to say." I felt her juices dripping down my legs, she started to shake and I knew she was about to cum. I grabbed a tight hold on her hips and leaned forward, biting her neck.

"Uhhh," she moaned while shaking uncontrollably like she was having a seizure. Two strokes later, I was right behind her, releasing my seeds inside her.

If I wasn't holding her up, she would have fallen right on her face. I laughed at her and shook my head. "If I was out fucking another bitch, I wouldn't have been able to fuck you like that," I said.

She was finally able to stand and someway, somehow she found the nerve to speak again. "Shut the hell up," she said, walking slowly to the shower.

"I love you too," I laughed, walking behind her. We washed each other's bodies before getting out of the shower. After we got dressed, she was on her way out the door with Amyricale and I went down to the basement to watch a movie on the big screen.

Reneice

I didn't know where Mykell ran his ass off to this morning, nor did I know what he was doing, but after the way he put it down, I didn't even care anymore. Maybe it's just my own insecurities or thoughts of the past, but whatever it is, I need to get over it. We've been doing good so far and I'm not trying to mess that up.

Amyricale and I walked into Town Kitchen & Bar and noticed Janae was already sitting at a table. When we reached the table, she stood and gave us a hug.

"Hey boo, you look like you haven't slept in days," I said.

"Honestly, I haven't. I'm so stressed out, it don't make no sense." She shook her head.

"You know you could have stayed at the house with us instead of going to a hotel."

"I know, but I needed some time to myself to think and figure some things out."

"I understand. So when is your appointment for the DNA test?" I asked as the waiter come to take our drink order.

"Thursday," she sighed.

"Are you nervous?" I asked.

"No, I know deep down inside that she's not Bishop's daughter. I mean…I understand why he questioned it and why he wants a test, but she just can't be his," she said as her eyes watered.

I got up and sat in the chair by her. "Don't cry boo, it's going to be okay. No matter what, you know Imma be here for you," I said as I hugged her.

"No cry Auntie Nae. Mommy make feel better," Amyricale said with a smile and we couldn't help but to laugh at her.

"I see that got a smile out of you," I chuckled.

"Yea, but enough about me. I see you've been very busy." She pointed to my neck.

I looked confused and she pulled out her compact mirror and handed it to me. I noticed a big hickey on the side of my neck, courtesy of Mykell. Janae laughed and Amyricale was trying to figure out what was so funny. “Keep playing around and yo ass gone end up pregnant again.”

“Too late for that,” I mumbled.

“Say what now?” she asked with a raised eyebrow.

I just looked at her and smiled. “No shit, how far along?” she asked, shocked.

“Five months,” I sighed.

“Why are you just now telling me? What the hell?” she fake pouted.

“I haven’t told anybody. I found out when I was…” I looked over at Amyricale and she was too busy playing on her iPad.

“Kell is going to flip if you don’t tell him soon.”

“I know, I’m going to tell him really, really soon.”

“You better girl.”

“I know, I am. I think he suspects something anyways because he poked me in my stomach today.” I laughed.

“Yup, his ass know.” She laughed.

Chapter 7

Mykell

I was out signing the last bit of paperwork I needed for Neicey's present. It wasn't a special occasion but I wanted to get her something anyway. I know she'll love it when she sees it. I walked out to my car and noticed I had left my phone in the car. I had eight missed calls from MJ. I hurried and dialed his number back to see what was so urgent.

Before I could even say anything his voiced boomed through the phone. "Pops, get to the hospital and get here now."

"What's wrong?" I asked.

"Me and Chyanne walked in the house and saw ma lying on the floor so I called the ambulance and they took her to the hospital. I got the kids with me, so don't worry about them. Just get here," said MJ.

"I'm coming now."

My mind was in overdrive trying to figure out what was wrong. I know before I left she said she didn't feel good, but she said it was nothing major. Now I feel like shit because I left her there by herself. I did 80 all the way to the hospital and I'm surprised I didn't get pulled over.

"I'm here to see my wife…Reneice Jones," I said to the nurse at the front desk.

"Room six. Take a left at the end of the hallway," she said after typing something in the computer.

I rushed down the hallway. This shit felt like déjà vu. The last time I was in the hospital to see Neicey, she was lying in a damn coma. I knocked on the door before going in; she was laid in the bed and smiled at me. The nurse was writing something down on a clipboard.

"Hey baby," she said faintly.

"What happened?" I asked.

"Her blood pressure was sky high and she fainted for a little. We want to keep her here for a few days so we can monitor her and the baby. She's at a high risk for having a miscarriage right now. We are doing everything we can to lower her blood pressure."

Baby? Miscarriage? What the hell? My mind was all over the place.

"Ma, me and Chy are about to take the kids to get something to eat. We'll be back later," MJ said.

"Alright."

When everyone left I walked over to sit by her bed. "How far along are you?" I asked. She said something, but I don't think that I heard her right. "Repeat that?" I said.

She sighed. "Five months, Mykell."

"Damn okay so when were you going to tell me?" I asked, trying not to get mad.

She looked away and didn't say anything. I just looked at her, staring a hole in the side of her face. All this talking I been doing about knocking her ass up and she been pregnant the whole time. I should be jumping for joy right now but I can't for the simple act that she kept it from me.

"Wow, I thought we were better than that," I said. "Why every time you get pregnant, it take some crazy shit to happen for me to find out?" I questioned.

"It don't," she whispered.

"Bullshit! The day you walked in my house waving a gun is the same day I found out you were pregnant with Romell. The same day I came down here to save yo ass, I found out you were pregnant with Amyricale, which happens to be the same day she was born. Then now, it took for you to damn near lose the baby for me to find out about it. What type of bullshit you be on?"

This shit was really bugging me out. I don't know whether to be happy or mad about the situation. There is still has a chance for survival, but she told have told me as soon as she found out about it. *Five months though?*

"I'm sorry," she broke down crying.

No matter how mad I am, I don't want to see my baby cry. I wiped her tears away and kissed her. "Don't cry. You know I hate seeing you cry," I said.

"I've just been so stressed out lately and I haven't had time to even really take care of myself because since I've been out, I've been taking care of everybody else," she said.

"I know, but I need for you to take care of you and the baby. Don't be eating nothing that's gon have you blood pressure sky high and don't let nothing stress you out. Not the kids, not the family, hell not even me." I smiled.

"I love you," she said, looking me in my eyes.

"I love you more." I kissed her again. I rubbed my hands on her belly. "See, I knew something was up because the other day, I noticed you was getting a little gut." I smirked.

She laughed and hit my arm. "Shut up."

"I got you something," I said.

"What is it?" she asked.

"Wouldn't you like to know?" I teased.

"Mykelllll," she whined.

I laughed at her, "I can't tell you, it's a surprise."

"I guess," she sighed.

The kids walked back through the door and I smiled looking at my family. Adding one more wouldn't hurt.

Ramone

I didn't know what's wrong with Le'Lani, but she had been on some bullshit since I went down to Florida. Every time I stepped in a room, she would get up and walk out; every time I tried to talk to her, she would ignore me. I've been calling her to see if I could get my daughter but she acted like she couldn't answer the phone. I knew she back in Michigan because Mykell already told me. *What the fuck is up with her?*

I was shaken from my thoughts by my girl Maya. "What you want to eat sexy?" she asked.

"Surprise me." I smiled.

Maya has been a big factor in my keeping my mind off of Lani and her bullshit. She's mad at me like I'm the one who went and got pregnant by another nigga. I mean, I know I'm wrong for telling her to get out, but I was hurt. Now she wanted to act like we couldn't even be friends, despite the fact that we were together for a minute and shared a child together.

I was sitting in the kitchen with Maya when my phone started ringing. It was a number that I didn't recognize but I went ahead and answered it anyway. "Hello?"

"Is this Ramone Peake?" a man asked.

"May I ask who's calling?"

"This is Dr. Lansky from Henry Ford Hospital," he said.

"Okay, how can I help you?" I questioned.

"Well Mr. Peake, I'm calling in regards to a paternity test you had done here. I was informed that one of my nurses mixed up some results behind some form of payment. Now, I can assure you that type of behavior is not acceptable and that nurse has been punished and no longer works here," he said.

My head was spinning. The only person that I had recently had a DNA done on was Zyla and that was almost two years ago. "So what are you saying doctor?" I asked confused.

"I'm calling to tell you to disregard the results for a...Zyla Moore because they are inaccurate and if you would like, we can do another test and I will do it personally, myself," he informed me.

"Uhh...Thank you. Is it alright if I call you back? I need some time to think this through."

"That will be no problem at all."

After I hung up the phone, I was stuck on stupid. My mind drifted back to a conversation I had with Ladybug when I was in Florida.

Ladybug was sitting in the living room watching TV. She held a sleeping Zyla in her hands and when she noticed me, she told me to come over to her.

"What's up, Ladybug?"

"I need to show you something that kind of freaked me out." She moved one of Zyla's ponytails

from her left ear and showed me a moon shaped birthmark that resembled the one I have. I stared at it for a few, but then shook it off.

"That's crazy huh?" she asked.

I sighed. "That don't mean nothing, Ladybug. Ranyla doesn't have one and I know for sure she's my daughter," I said.

"I'm saying Mone, maybe you need to get her tested again. That's kind of hard to explain. Why you two have the same exact birthmark in the same exact place?" she said.

"I know but we already tested her and the results proved that she was 99.9% not mine."

"But Mone—"

"Drop it Ladybug."

Now I sat there thinking I should have listened to my sister. I tried dialing Lani's number one more time, but I still didn't get an answer. I knew the two people I could talk to if I couldn't talk to anybody else.

* * *

I pulled up to Pops' house and was happy that my dad had beaten me here because I needed to talk to the both of them ASAP. Pops must have heard me pull up because as soon as I pulled up, he opened the front door for me.

"Wassup Pops?"

"You tell me. You said it was very important so let's not bullshit and get straight to it," he said. My dad sat up on the couch, giving me his undivided attention.

I took a deep breath before starting, "Okay, so I got a call from the doctor at the hospital that Zyla was born at. He tells me how once of his nurses confessed that she was paid to mix up the results of the DNA test. He wants to disregard the results we have and come do another test," I said all in one breath.

They both sat there looking at me like I was crazy. They were driving me crazy, I needed one of them to say something and say something fast. "Well…" I said.

My dad was the first one to say something. "I'm saying, do you really want to open that door again? How do we know that somebody else won't fuck up the results?" he asked.

"That's the same thing I was thinking, but the doctor assured me that he would be handling it personally if we chose to do it."

Pops decided to speak this time. "Have you talked to my daughter? I think this could either put your mind at ease or cause more of a strain on your relationship."

"I've been calling Le'Lani for a week straight and she won't answer. I don't know what's wrong with her, but she needs to get over it real fast because I'm tired of playing these games with her."

"I'll talk to her; in the meantime I just need for you to figure out what you want to do if you don't already know," he said.

Right then, my mind was all over the place. This situation was the exact same thing that tore us apart. If I found out that Zyla is actually mine, will it bring us back together? Do I want us to get back together? Will *she* want to get back together? This is starting to be a little too much for me.

Pop-Pop

I need a damn vacation. These kids are going to send me to an early grave. I noticed a gray hair growing the other day and that is not acceptable, I'm too young, fly and sexy for all that. My kids are in a lot of shit right now from paternity issues to being stalked by lawyers; on top of that, MJ's ass possibly could have made me a GREAT-grandfather. What type of shit is that? It was so much easier to deal with these issues when we all lived in the same place, but Neicey and Mykell just had to run they asses down south.

The one I'm worried about the most is my baby girl, Le'Lani. She liked to go MIA, not answer her phone or call nobody for weeks at a time and I didn't like that shit. I told her a long time ago that nigga wasn't no good for her. I know I have to let her make her own mistakes and learn from them but what she needs to realize is, I'm her daddy and I wouldn't lie to her. She can talk to me about whatever is going on, but she would rather be a hard ass about it. She reminds me so much of her mother, it's crazy.

I grabbed the phone and dialed her number hoping that she would answer. It rang five times and right when I was about to hang up, she answered.

"Hi daddy," she said softly. That sent up a red flag because Lani is the farthest thing from quiet or soft-spoken.

"Oh, so you know who I am? And you recognize my number?" I asked sarcastically.

"Don't go there daddy, I've been meaning to call you. I've just been real busy, but then I got a crazy ass phone call so I'm stressed."

"That phone call is what I want to talk to you about."

"How do you know what phone call I'm talking about?" she asked.

"Ramone came to see me. So what are you going to do now that you know what happened?" I asked.

She sighed. "I already knew," she admitted.

I took the phone away from my ear thinking I heard her wrong. "Say that again?" I said.

"Zamier told me he paid to have the results mixed up a couple of weeks ago."

I thought that my daughter had officially lost her damn mind. I took a deep breath to keep me from saying everything I wanted to say. I felt my temper rising, so I changed the subject. "When you coming to see me?" I asked.

"I promise I'll come see you when I get the time," she said.

"Well damn, I have to make an appointment to see my own daughter now?" I asked, half-jokingly.

"Daddy," she whined.

"Alright Le'Lani, I'm just messing with you. Call me when you can," I said.

"Okay daddy, love you."

"I love you too."

I just shook my head. I wasn't too worried about what's going on with her because sooner rather than later, it would come to the light and I had a very funny feeling that the shit was going to hit the ceiling fan.

Lani

It had been a living hell since I'd been back in Michigan. I really wished I would have listened to Mykell when he told me not to come back, but there were just some things I had to take care of before I just up and moved down there. At least I haven't seen or heard from Zamier since I've been here and that's a plus. My brother had thought I ran back up here to be with him but I had to let him know that that was not the case.

Since I've been back, the girls and I have been staying at a hotel. Since Nyla is older, she liked to ask a lot of questions, she wanted to know why we're not staying at the house and I kept having to tell her that we weren't staying here that long, so this was only a temporary thing.

We had just left from getting the girls some ice cream and I was running low on gas so I stopped by the gas station. Ranyla just insisted in going into the gas station with me so that she could pay and feel like a big girl. I took her out and grabbed Zyla. While I was unbuckling Zyla, I heard Ranyla scream.

"Daddy!" I looked up to see her running to Ramone. He looked shocked at first then smiled when he noticed his daughter. I rolled my eyes, *I don't need this shit right now.* I took Zyla out and put her on my hip. I looked up and noticed some light skinned chick standing extra close to Ramone and grinning at Nyla.

I walked right past him like he didn't exist and went to pay for the gas. From inside, I could tell Ranyla was asking him who the girl was. I wanted to know myself but I already knew our daughter would give me the run down. After I was done, I walked out and tried to walk past him again but he stopped me this time. It was the middle of November and too chilly to be standing here socializing.

"Nyla, hug your daddy bye and get in the car," I said, not looking at him.

Zyla smiled and reached for Ramone and he reached his arm out for her but I turned her from him and walked away, headed towards my car. Ain't no way in hell I was going to let him touch my daughter after all this time when he was acting funny towards her and mistreating her. Now that she could possibly be his, he wants to hold her. *He can go to hell.* I thought as strapped Zyla back in her car seat.

"Le'Lani!" Ramone said, walking up to me with Ranyla in his arms. I ignored him and walked to the pump to get my gas and leave.

"Nyla, I said get in the car. Tell your daddy you gotta go," I said.

"Bye daddy," she said sadly.

"Bye princess," he said kissing her. She got out of his arms and got in the car.

"Lani look…" he started but stopped when the girl that was standing by him earlier walked up.

"Hi, I'm Maya," she said and reached her hand out. I looked at her hand then back at the monitor making sure I didn't go over my amount. "So you're Lani, huh?" she asked like she was amused.

"It looks that way, don't it?" I said, looking her up and down. My eyes shifted to Ramone and he was standing there looking like a lost puppy. After I was done, I walked past both of them and got in the car. I tried to shut the door but Ramone grabbed it.

"I want to see my daughters Le'Lani," he said.

I laughed. This nigga is a trip, now all of a sudden Zyla is his daughter. “You mean daughter? You see Ranyla right now don’t you? As far as Zyla goes, she has a daddy and don’t need another one. Now move, I have some place I need to be and your girl is waiting on you,” I said, shutting the door and pulling out of the gas station in the Beamer he bought me without looking back.

As soon as we got back to the hotel, I called Mykell and vented. He’s the only person I’ve been talking to because he’s the only person that knows my situation. He’s been making good on his promise by not telling anybody. I know it’s killing him not to say anything, but it’s for the best.

“I’m telling you Kell, that nigga ain’t shit!” I fumed pacing back and forth.

“Lani, calm down. You said it yourself that he didn’t introduce you two; she had to do it herself, so what that tell you?” he asked.

“That tells me that his ass was stuck on stupid because he wasn’t expecting to have to tell me. Nyla already told me that the bitch introduced herself as her daddy girlfriend. I’m not even mad about that because I’m not even feeling him right now. I’m mad because he went crazy on me for moving on with Zamier and moving in with him, but he goes and gets a new bitch.”

“Baby girl, listen to me, she is only a temporary thing. You know all you have to do is play yo role and that nigga will be yours again.”

I took the phone away from my ear and looked at it crazy, thinking Mykell could see me. "Mykell, did you not hear me the first time I said it? I do not want him; I'm so over him and his shit right now."

"Whatever, but look, Neicey want y'all to come down here for Thanksgiving. She wants the whole family down here so that means you too. That's only four damn days away so bring ya ass down here, Le'Lani. I don't want to have to come show my ass," he said.

I laughed at his goofy ass. Leave it up to him to say something to make me laugh when I'm pissed. "Alright I'm coming....I love you Kell," I said to my brother.

"Tell me something I don't know." Mykell laughed. "Naw but I love you too, knucklehead."

After I got off the phone with my brother, my phone started ringing again. I looked down to see Zamier's name pop up. I thought that was weird because I haven't spoken to him in weeks. Against my better judgment, I answered it. "Hello?"

"He's gone Lani! They fucking killed him!" his voice boomed through the phone.

"Wait, slow down. Who are you talking about?" I asked, confused.

"They fucking killed Marco and I didn't even have a chance to save him," he cried.

"Calm down, where are you?" I was really concerned. I had grown real fond of Marco. He was a great friend to Neicey when she needed him and he was a real cool down to earth dude.

"I'm at the house. I need you Lani, I fucking need you," he cried some more.

I sighed, I was conflicted. I wanted to stay far away from him as possible. *It won't hurt to see him for a few minutes.* "I'm on my way." I had plans of going in, saying some kind words and getting out.

* * *

When I got to the house it smelled like a damn liquor store. All the lights were off and it was pitch black. I was carrying a sleeping Zyla in my arms and Ranyla was holding my hand tightly. "Mommy, I can't see," she said.

"Hold on baby." I went to turn the light on and damn near jumped out of my skin when I saw Zamier sitting on the couch cradling a Hennessey bottle. I walked upstairs and laid Zyla down then turned on cartoons for Ranyla in their old rooms.

I came back downstairs and could tell that he was drunk already. The bottle was more than halfway empty and I didn't want to get too close to him because his ass turns into a different person when he gets drunk.

Before I could even open my mouth, Zamier spoke. "They shot my damn cousin down like he was a damn dog. He wasn't doing nothing but minding his own business and they took him from me. I couldn't even react because by time it started it was already over," he said looking at me. "I would have been able to react if my mind wasn't fucked up," he said, getting up and dropping the liquor bottle in the process.

"What are you talking about?" I asked getting defensive.

"If yo ass knew how to act instead of being so fucking stupid, my mind would have been right," he said as he lunged towards me. I tried to run but he grabbed me by the hair.

"Zamier stop! You're fucking drunk!" I yelled in pain. His hold was so tight, it felt like my hair was about to detach from my scalp.

He pulled be back and slapped the shit out of me. "You told that nigga about Zyla? Huh?" he said, slapping me again.

"WHAT THE FUCK ARE YOU TALKING ABOUT?!" I screamed.

He pushed me down and I tried to crawl to the broken glass on the floor but he kicked me in my back. I fell to the ground and he just started punching me. I reached my hand out and grabbed a piece of the glass and reached back and sliced. I didn't care where I cut him just as long as I got him.

"AHH!" he screamed.

I hadn't noticed Ranyla came down the stairs until I heard her screaming. I looked back to see that he had her by her hair. I grabbed one of the lamps and hit him in the head right when he was about to hit her. He hit the ground with a big thump. I grabbed a crying

Ranyla and kissed her. “Baby, go run outside and get in the car. I left the door unlocked.” She nodded her head and ran out the door.

I ran up the stairs and grabbed Zyla and ran back down the stairs. I felt for a pulse and he still had one. *Good, I’ll let Mykell kill him,* I thought, running to the car with my daughter. I sped out of the driveway, heading straight for the highway. Florida here I come.

I didn’t give a fuck about what that nigga may do to me but he fucked up when he touched my daughter.

Chapter 8

Mykell

"All that shit you was talking and you can't handle it," Neicey said as she rode me like a professional cowgirl.

I didn't know what has gotten into her, but ever since she got home from the hospital, she had been on some freak shit. Shit, I would never complain at all. I actually love the shit. We'd been going at it for about two hours and her ass didn't seem like she wanna stop anytime soon.

I smacked her ass. "Shut the fuck up."

She giggled and sped up. I felt her muscles getting tighter and knew she was about to explode. I grabbed her hips and pounded into her. "Uhhhh, wa..waaaaait!" she moaned.

"Naw, what's all that shit you was talking huh?" I smiled when I felt her juices dripping down my dick. I kept pumping and finally bust inside her. She fell forward on my chest trying to catch her breath. She rolled over and lay on her back, breathing hard. My phone had started ringing and since she was closer she picked it up. Her face screwed up and her mouth flew open.

Next thing I know, I felt a slap across my face. I grabbed my face and looked at her like she was crazy. She tried to swing again but I grabbed her wrist and pinned her down on the bed. “What the fuck is yo problem?” I yelled.

If looks could kill, I would have dropped dead on the spot. Her chest was heaving up and down and was looking like she was ready to kill my ass. “You fucking that bitch?” she questioned through gritted teeth.

I tilted my head to the side. “Who the fuck is you talking about Reneice?” I asked, pissed off. I had just busted me a good ass nut, now she wanna come at me on some bullshit.

“Don’t play dumb, you know who the fuck I’m talking about,” she said with tears in her eyes. “After everything we’ve been through, that’s how you do me?” she cried.

I put both her wrists together and held them with my right hand while I grabbed my phone with my left hand. *What the fuck?* Toni’s nutty ass had the nerve to send me a damn nude picture.

I threw the phone on the bed and looked at Reneice but she wouldn’t look at me. “Let me up Mykell,” she said.

“Fuck that, look I am not fucking that bitch.” I grabbed her face and made her look at me before I kept talking. “I put that on my mama and our first child that I am not fucking that bitch. Her crazy ass been stalking me since I hired her ass to be your lawyer. She even threatened that if I didn’t fuck her she would have made sure you went to prison for life. But I didn’t do it. I already told you before I made you my wife that I was going to do right by you and I meant that shit.”

I grabbed my phone and went to Toni's messages in my phone. "Look, not once did I reply to her crazy ass," I said, handing her my phone. I let her up to look at the messages.

After reading them all, she looked at me with fire in her eyes. "Why didn't you tell me? That shit looks real suspect since you kept it from me," she said.

"Because I knew if I told you, yo crazy ass would have went after her. You just got off for a damn double murder charge and I was not about to let you go back. The only reason I'm telling you now is because I don't want you stressing and thinking I'm fucking her when I'm not," I said.

She didn't respond, instead she pressed a button on the phone. I knew that she called Toni because she had the phone on speaker. I wanted to stop her but that could be deadly on my behalf.

"I knew you would like my message. Wifey must not be around, I'm tired of you playing and fighting it Mykell. I know you want me. I won't tell if you don't."

This bitch is beyond crazy.

"Look bitch, I'm only going to tell you this one time and one time only. You better leave my husband alone. It's a lot of things in this world that I play around with but he's not one of them. Now, I'm going the nice route and telling you nicely, next time I'll be putting a bullet in you," Neicey said before hanging up.

It wasn't what she said but how she said it that gave me a chill. She got up and walked to the bathroom but stopped at the door. “Come on,” she said before going in.

We bathed each other then got out. Before I stepped out, she kissed me. “I’m sorry,” she said. “I shouldn’t have hit you or jumped to conclusions.”

“It’s cool. I’m not tripping about it because I know how it looked. But I need for you to learn how to trust me. I know I did some fucked up shit in the past but we’re over that. Or at least I thought we were. I’ve been thinking, maybe we need to go see a marriage counselor.”

She looked at me funny. “People only need them if their thinking about getting a divorce,” she said.

“Hit my ass like that again, and I will divorce yo ass,” I joked.

“Whatever boy, you ain’t going nowhere.” She smiled while getting dressed.

“Yea whatever,” I laughed.

The doorbell rang and we gave each other a look, wondering who it could be.

“You finish getting dressed and I’ll see who that is,” Neicey said.

Right when I finished buckling my pants, I heard Neicey scream my name. *Ah shit.* I thought as I ran down the stairs.

Reneice

I damn near lost my mind when I opened the door and saw Lani standing there with her face swollen. My mind was going 100 mph trying to figure out what the hell happened.

"Mykell!" I yelled.

"I'm sorry Neicey, he was going to kill me. He tried to hit Nyla and I lost it, I fucking lost it," she said.

"Shhhh, baby it's okay," I said, taking Zyla out her arms.

Mykell came running down the stairs like a damn maniac. "What the fuck!" he yelled.

I took Ranyla by the hand and led her up the stairs. I laid Zyla down in Amyricale's bed and turned on some cartoons for Nyla.

"You hungry baby?" I asked her.

"Yes TT," she said.

"Alright lil mama, I'm going to go make us lunch," I said, kissing her forehead.

Before I could walk out the room, she stopped me. "TT."

"Yea baby?"

"Is Z going to follow us here and get us? He whooped mommy and I'm scared. I want my daddy," she said.

"Don't worry baby, he's not going to come here. I promise you that." I smiled.

When I went back downstairs, Mykell was pacing back on forth while talking on the phone. Lani was sitting on the couch with ice in her face. I walked over to her and her mouth hit the floor. "Oh my God, Neicey, your stomach! When did this happen?" she asked.

"Surprise," I laughed. "I was going to tell everyone on Thanksgiving." I smiled.

"I'm happy for y'all." She smiled.

"Thanks boo, but enough about me. When were you going to tell me? Why didn't you say anything?" I asked as I examined her face.

Before she could answer, Mykell had a damn outburst. "I'm telling you Mack, that nigga better off himself if he knows what's good for him because Imma make sure he die a slow painful death!" he yelled.

We knew better than to say anything when he's pissed off, so we just let him rant. Lani sighed. "I told Kell before you came home. I made him promise that he wasn't going to say anything and in return I wouldn't go back to him."

"So this is not the first time? So it has happened more than once?" I asked getting mad.

She nodded. I bolted up the stairs and went to the back of the closet and grabbed my newly bought gun. I made sure my nickel plated .45 was loaded. I turned around to walk out the closet but bumped into Mykell.

“What the hell you think you doing and where the hell you think you going? No, fuck all that. How the hell do you keep getting these damn guns?” he asked, taking my gun from me.

“Really? Why the hell didn’t you tell me that nigga was beating on Le’Lani? What the fuck part of the game is that?” I asked.

“Calm yo ass down! She said she wasn’t going back to his ass but trust me when I say I was already planning his death the moment she walked through my door with a busted lip the first time. What I don’t need is for my pregnant wife going and setting shit off,” he said, pulling me out the closet.

“Mykell, our niece is in the other room scared as hell thinking Zamier is going to follow them here and get her. She said he whooped her mommy. Now that shit is bothering me like hell. Ramone is going to have a damn fit when he finds this shit out.”

“Baby look at me, I got this. You know good and damn well I am not about to let that nigga hurt her no more.”

I sighed knowing her meant what he said. The only thing I could do now is just sit back and let my husband be the man. “Alright, I have to go run to the store and get the food and stuff for Thanksgiving. The kids should be back in a minute.”

He leaned down and kissed me. “Be careful and be safe.”

I smiled. “I will.”

* * *

As soon as I got in the car, my phone rang. Thinking it was Mykell calling to tell me to grab him something, I answered without looking. “Yes, Love?” I answered pulling out of the driveway.

“Neicey…”

It can’t be. I thought as I looked at the number on my phone. “Why are you calling me Kamil?” I asked.

“Neicey, please, I just want to talk to you.”

“I think you said everything you needed to say in that letter. I can’t believe you would do some crazy shit like that Kamil,” I fumed.

“Can you please just meet up with me? I want to apologize in person.”

I hesitated for a minute. Knowing that it wasn’t a good idea and that Mykell would lose his damn mind if he found out, I took in a deep breath. “Where are you?”

“I’m at the Tropical Park.”

“Alright, I’m on my way.”

When I pulled up to the park, I pulled my phone out of my purse to call Kamil back and tell him I was there.

Tap Tap Tap

I damn near jumped out of my skin when I heard somebody tapping on my window. Kamil was standing there, smiling like the shit was funny.

I got out of the car with a scowl on my face. "Boy, you almost got shot. What the hell is wrong with you?" I asked.

He snickered. "I'm happy to see you too."

I looked him up and down and I'd be lying if said he didn't look good; he looked damn good. He was standing there in a wife beater, some dark blue jeans, and some Timberlands even though it was damn near eighty degrees out. He had let his hair grow out and it was curly, his beard was trimmed. His thug appeal was turning me on. *Damn, Neicey snap out of it.*

"I see you checking me out," he smiled.

"Why the hell did you have to show up looking so damn good?" I said, faking an attitude.

"Only for you," he said and I rolled my eyes.

"Get to talking," I said, folding my arms.

He sighed and took a cigarette out his back pocket and lit it. He inhaled the smoke then exhaled it.

"So we smoking squares now?" I asked.

"A nigga been stressed lately." He shrugged. "But all bullshit aside, I know that shit I did was wrong and I know sorry not gon cut it. I never thought about how my decision would affect you and I was being selfish. I owe you an apology because I can just imagine the shit you had to go through because of me," he said looking me in the eyes.

I hated when he did that shit only because I could see how sincere he was. I didn't want to forgive him, not like I always did.

"You know, I had intentions of putting a bullet in yo ass when I saw you after I read your letter. I'm sorry if you felt like I was stringing you along or using you, but that was never the fact. I do love you and I appreciate everything you've done for me. You were there for me when I needed you the most. I know you don't understand it and probably never will but I'm in love with Mykell. We've had a crazy ass relationship and everything we have been through made our relationship stronger."

He nodded his head in understanding. "I hear what you saying and once again I apologize."

I smiled and kissed him softly on his lips. "Naw, I need for you to get far away from here and go somewhere his crazy ass won't find you because they've already put two and two together and know it was you," I warned.

"It's already in motion. I just wanted to talk to you before I left for good."

I opened my car door and got in. "Bye Mil Mil." I smiled.

"Bye baby girl."

I let out a big breath. That went better than I expected. I pulled out the park and went to my original destination, to do some grocery shopping. *If I wasn't so crazy in love with Mykell, he could have been the one. Maybe….*

MJ

Things between me and Chyanne have not been going too good lately. I don't know if it's the pregnancy hormones or what, but she's been very moody. I've been around my mom every time she was pregnant and it was enough to know the signs and my dad just let her have her way so that's what I did with Chyanne.

We haven't spoken in a few days, so I called and told her that I wanted to take her to the movies and spend some time with her. I love being around her, she's cool, laid back, goofy and I can just chill and be myself around her. I know I'm only a teenager but the multiple female thing ain't for me. I had seen my dad go through that shit and I didn't ever want to go through what he did. That takes too much of my energy.

I pulled up to our old condo and saw Chyanne standing there looking beautiful. I mean, it wasn't just what she had on, but her glow made her even more beautiful. I noticed some dude was all up in her face and she was grinning from ear to damn ear.

I sat there and played it cool for a minute. When she finally noticed me, she smiled real big and said her goodbyes to the dude. She walked over to the car and I noticed just how short her shorts really were.

"Hey baby," she kissed my cheek.

I just cut my eyes at her without responding and pulled out of the parking lot. I turned my music all the way so she would catch the hint that I didn't want to talk. She reached for the knob and turned the music down and I looked at her like she was crazy before returning my attention back to the road.

"What's wrong with you?" she asked.

I ignored her for a few before finally answering her. "You know what? I don't even feel like watching a movie no more," I said hitting a U-turn and heading back to my house.

She smacked her lips and turned the music back up. The rest of the ride to the house was silent besides the radio. When I pulled in the driveway, I hopped out of the car and headed straight to the front door, not even waiting on Chyanne.

My mom and dad were sitting on the couch chilling when I walked in and I plopped down on the couch across from them. They both looked at me like I was crazy. "What?" I asked.

"The hell you mean what nigga? You supposed to be at the movies, so what the hell are you doing here?" my dad asked.

Before I could even ask, Chyanne waddled her pregnant ass in the house and rolled her eyes at me. "Hey ma and dad," she spoke before going upstairs.

My mom looked at her then looked back at me and shook her head. “I don’t even want to hear it MJ, I swear I don’t,” she said shaking her head.

“I didn’t do nothing, Ma. She the one who had a nigga smiling all in her face and shit,” I said.

“Watch yo mouth.” She cut her eyes at me.

“Sorry, but that’s disrespectful,” I said.

My dad chuckled like somebody said a joke or something and I wanted to know what was funny. “What’s so funny?” I asked.

“You lil nigga, how the hell you gon get mad because she was talking to another dude and you talk to other girls?” he laughed.

“Because that’s different. How would you feel if you saw some dude all up in mom’s face, then she gets in the car all happy like ain’t shit happen?”

“Oh God. Mykell please talk to your son.” My mom rolled her eyes.

“My pleasure,” he sat up. “I would be flattered that another nigga was all up in her face because she’s a bad bitch.” He smiled but it didn’t last long because mom slapped him in the back of the head.

He looked at her like he didn’t know what he did and I just laughed at the two of them. “What he’s trying to say, MJ, is that Chyanne is beautiful so of course other boys are going to want her. You should be happy that she chose to be with *you* because that means you have something that they want but can't get. Have you forgotten that she is pregnant? I doubt that she's thinking about another nigga," my mom said.

Everything she just said made a lot of sense. I overreacted for nothing, knowing Chyanne not that type of girl. I sighed before getting up to apologize. I went upstairs to find Amyricale and Ranyla in my room with Chyanne. I smiled at the three of them, MyMy is such a charmer and adorable. I can already tell Imma have to be hard on her when she gets older.

"What's up princess?" I said after diving on my king size bed.

"MJ, I tell Chy Chy about my American girl doll. NyNy got one too!" she said excitedly.

"Really?" I asked.

"Yes." She nodded.

Ranyla was rubbing Chyanne's belly and smiling. "I hope it's a girl so me and MyMy can play with her," she told Chyanne.

"Nyla, why you touching all on my baby? Huh?" I asked while grabbing and tickling her. She started cracking up laughing and Amyricale jumped on my back telling me to leave her cousin alone.

"What are you two doing?" my auntie Lani asked smiling.

"Mommy help!" Ranyla yelled.

"Alright Mykell Jr., you better leave my baby alone," she threatened jokingly.

I laughed and let Ranyla go. She jumped of the bed and ran to her mom. "C'mon Amyricale, I need you and Nyla to help me pick Zyla out something to wear," she said. The two of them ran out of the room happily and when I turned to Chyanne, I could tell she was mad at me.

I decided to do what my dad does when mom is mad at him. I scooted over to her and rubbed on her belly and kissed her neck. "Chy Chy," I said.

"Leave me alone Mykell Jr.," she said.

I knew she was mad then because that's the only time she calls me by my government name. I started sucking on her neck and her breathing started to speed up. "I'm sorry," I whispered.

"You not slick," she laughed and pushed me away.

"For real, I'm sorry. I shouldn't have acted like that, you forgive me?" I fake pouted.

"I'll think about it," she joked.

I grabbed her and pulled her down on the bed with me. I kissed her cheek before lifting up her shirt and kissing her on the stomach. "I love y'all."

"I love you too," she said, then tears started falling.

I wiped them away, “What’s wrong?” I asked concerned.

“I’m scared, what if this baby comes out not to be yours? I’ll feel so bad because I’m stringing you along and I never wanted to be one of those females who didn’t know who the father of her child is,” she cried. “I’m just another damn statistic.”

“Chyanne, go ahead with all that shit. I already told you regardless of the results, that’s still my baby. I don’t give a damn how young we are, I’m still taking care of that baby regardless. And fuck being a damn statistic! You are not no damn statistic so don’t let me hear you say that,” I said.

She just nodded her head.

“Knock, Knock.” I turned around to see my dad standing there. “Chyanne, somebody’s here to see you,” he said.

She looked confused then got up to see who it was. My dad smiled at me. “I raised a damn solider,” he smiled.

We heard some yelling and rushed down stairs to see what was going on.

Chyanne

When I got downstairs, I was shocked to see my mom at the door. I knew this couldn’t be a good thing because Mama Neicey looked like she was ready to kill.

I haven't spoken to my mom in weeks, so I was wondering what she was doing here and how she knew where I was.

"Mom, what are you doing here and what do you want?" I asked.

"I want you to come get the rest of your shit out my house or it will be in the garbage. Let these people take care of you since this is where you want to be!" she yelled while walking up on me.

Mama Neicey jumped in front of me and pushed me back, "Hold the fuck up, you better watch yo damn tone in my house and watch who you talking to. I don't play that," she said.

"I don't give a damn, this is my daughter," she said.

"I can't tell bitch," Mama Neicey said.

Then all of a sudden I noticed my dad walk in and instantly I started to shake in fear. I backed up and bumped into MJ on accident. I turned around to see fire in his eyes.

"Go upstairs Chyanne," he said without looking at me. "Ma, what the hell is he doing here?"

"Little nigga, I owe you a good ass whooping. That's what the fuck I'm doing here," my dad said. I just knew some shit was about to pop off.

"I wish like hell you would," Daddy Kell said.

I ran upstairs to go get Auntie Lani, but by the time I reached the top of the stairs, she was coming out of her room. "What's going on?" she asked.

"My mom and dad are here trying to start something," I said.

"Go in the room with the girls and take Tyriq and Fat Fat in there with you," she said.

I went to Tyriq's room and grabbed him before telling Romell to come on. We all stayed in there, I watched the girls as they played with their dolls, Romell and Tyriq played on their iPads and Zyla was sleep. I was a nervous wreck. I didn't want to go back to my mom and dad. I would rather stay where I am and be happy than to be miserable with them.

After what seemed like forever, Daddy Kell came and got me. "C'mon Chy Chy, you don't have to worry about shit, you're not going back with them and I told them that they can keep that shit and I'll buy you whatever you need." He hugged me.

I didn't want to cry but I did anyway. I don't know what I would do if it wasn't for MJ and his family.

Lakey

I was chilling on the couch smoking a blunt waiting for Daniella to get home. I didn't know why her ass insisted on working when I already told her she didn't have to, but she was one of them females that refused to let a nigga take care of her and I had no choice to respect it.

I know I got me a damn keeper. She's not like any of the females I've ever messed with. She don't be with all that drama shit but she has no problem with checking my ass if she feels like I'm fucking up. She's not insecure but she let bitches know that she's wifey and she's not going anywhere anytime soon. She done made a nigga like me fall for her and I fell hard.

I heard the keys turning and knew my baby was home. She walked in looking flawless as hell. She recently went to the salon and got her hair cut in a bob that went perfectly with her face. She smiled as she walked over to me and straddled my lap, she took the blunt out my hands and took a hit. She put her mouth to mine and gave me shotgun.

"What's up sexy, did you miss me?" she asked.

"Hell yea, now get in there and cook me something to eat woman," I laughed while slapping her ass.

"Whatever loser," she laughed while getting up.

"How was work?" I asked.

"Good, I'll be happy when Neicey can come work with me. I need some entertainment. I called Chyanne and told her to come in for an interview even though I already know I'm going to hire her," she said.

"That's what's up, but you know Kell is not about to let her ass work until she have that baby," I laughed.

"I know," she whined.

I sat back and watched her as she moved around the house. She's so beautiful to me. "Aye, LaLa!" I said as she walked in the kitchen.

"Yes big head?"

"I love you girl," I said.

She smiled real big, "I love you too."

"Oh, Neicey invited us to come over for Thanksgiving tomorrow. Is that cool with you?" I asked.

"Of course," she said before going back into the kitchen.

I picked up my phone to call MJ. He claimed he wanted to handle this Kamil situation but I haven't heard from him since the last time he came over.

"Wassup Unc?" he answered.

"That's what I'm trying to figure out Nephew, what's up with that situation?"

"I haven't had a chance to handle it, I been too busy with Chyanne and the baby thing," he sighed.

"I understand but it might be too late, I went over to the condo he was living in and it was completely empty. No trace of him at all," I said.

"Shit," he said. "His ass is slick."

"Yea, with his profession, you're supposed to move in silence and his ass is pretty good at that, but I'll talk to you tomorrow."

"Alright Unc, thanks for the info."

"No doubt," I said before hanging up.

Lani

I told Neicey that I would help her cook for Thanksgiving since she's pregnant, I don't want her on her feet that much. I took Chyanne with me to finish the last minute shopping for the stuff we still needed. Coming to Florida was exactly what I needed, it was a big breath of fresh air. I've been doing a lot of thinking about moving down here for good.

I took my eyes off of the road to glance at Chyanne, she's a very pretty girl but you can tell by the pain in her eyes that she's been through a lot. "So, have you and MJ thought of any baby names yet?" I asked.

"Well, if it's a girl, we were thinking Mikyah and if it's a boy, he wants to name him Mykell the Third."

"Oh Lord, we do not need another Mykell in this world, two of them is enough," I laughed.

"That's what Mama Neicey said," she laughed with me.

My heart damn near dropped when I noticed Ramone's Benz in the driveway when we pulled up. *I thought he wasn't coming until tomorrow,* I thought as I parked behind him. He was sitting on the porch on the bench swing with Zyla on his lap and I tried not to get an attitude. I knew Nyla wasn't too far behind because she's a daddy's girl to the heart.

Mykell and MJ came out of the house to help me and Chyanne with the bags. I walked on the porch and Zyla smiled and got happy. "Mama!" she said clapping her hands.

"Hey mama baby," I said bending down to kiss her.

"I think she needs a diaper change and hello to you too," Ramone said.

I rolled my eyes at him, took my daughter from him and walked in the house. Romell, Tyriq, Amyricale and Ranyla, and Keiyari were all in the den watching *Frozen*, I smiled because it's been so long since I've seen Keiyari and I missed him. I watched them for a little then headed up to the room I sleep in.

Zyla was trying to talk but I could only understand some of the words she was saying. She was in her terrible twos and into everything. "It's time for you to be potty trained lil mama," I said while undressing her.

She laughed like she was saying "yea right". I damn near jumped out of my skin when I felt something poke me in the ass. I turned around to see Ramone standing there all up in my personal space. "Back the hell up," I said with an attitude while pushing him.

"Why you got this damn dress on with no panties?" he asked.

I ignored him and continued to change Zyla's diaper. "Dada." She smiled at Ramone. I cut my eyes at him and he was smiling.

"I really need for you to stop playing with my daughters' emotions, that shit is not even cute," I said as I put her shorts back on.

"Nyla mama," she said with a pout.

"Go get her then," I said taking her down from the bed.

I put the diaper in the diaper dispenser in the bathroom, and before I could leave, I bumped into Ramone and he pushed me up against the wall. I was still sore, so that shit hurt. "Ahhh," I winced.

He turned me around and moved the top half of my dress and I tried to move away but he tightened his grip. "So I guess Kell wasn't lying huh?" he said with venom dripping from his voice.

"Leave it alone and drop it." I turned around to look at him in the eye to let him know that I was serious.

"Drop it huh? This nigga was beating on you and you want me to drop it? When were you going to tell me Le'Lani?"

"Why does it matter Ramone, I'm not your concern. The only person you need to be worried about is Ranyla Love Peake, not me," I said.

"It matters because I fucking love yo dumb ass and I'm willing to admit that I was wrong and I'm sorry," he said.

"So how did you end up with Keiyari and why didn't you bring Maya?" I said changing the subject. I really didn't have time for his bullshit.

He chuckled. "Carmen was sick and she asked me to take him."

"Okay…" I said.

"Okay what?" he shrugged.

"You didn't answer my other question," I said.

"Why do you care?" he asked.

"Because she need to come get her nigga and keep him the hell out my face," I said pushing him and walking out the bathroom. I rushed downstairs to find Neicey because I couldn't stand being around her brother for too much longer.

I found her in the kitchen with Chyanne and Daniella. "What's up mamas, can I help?" I asked.

"About time, I was wondering what was taking you so long, Zyla said you and her dada were talking," Neicey said trying to be funny.

"I'm not even about to go there with you right now, Reneice," I laughed.

"What? I didn't say anything. I'm just telling you what Zyla said." She smiled.

"Whatever you fat cow, it's too many pregnant women in here. I don't need that rubbing off on me. Daniella you better run before you be next," I joked.

"Yea right, Lakey been trying to knock my ass up for two weeks now." She laughed.

"Oh Lord, y'all got baby fever." I shook my head.

"Who got baby fever?" Janae asked walking into the kitchen.

"Aw shit, the party is about to get started now." I laughed.

I looked around the kitchen, happy that I was blessed to have these wonderful women in my life, Chyanne and Daniella included.

Chapter 9

Mykell

It was the morning of Thanksgiving and I had a lot to be thankful for. I still had breath in my body, I was a free man, I had my beautiful wife by my side, I had all my kids with me, all my family was here. What more could I ask for? I was deep in thought when Neicey turned over and looked at me.

"What you thinking about?" she asked.

I rubbed on her belly and kissed her. "You,"

"That's who you better be thinking about," she laughed.

I chuckled and bent down to kiss her belly. "Hey daddy's princess."

"I sure do hope it's a girl, it's too much damn testosterone in this house," she said.

"I agree. I feel like I be competing for your attention between Tyriq and Romell," I said.

She laughed. "Whatever, but I was thinking if it's a girl we can name her Kamora Cherice Jones. What you think?" she asked.

"I love it, especially the middle name."

"Yea I wanted to be a mixture of our mother's names," she said.

"That's nice baby," I said kissing her neck.

"Don't start something you can't finish, Mykell," she moaned.

"Oh. I have every intention on finishing."

Right after I said that, Tyriq decided it was a good time to bust into the room. *Dammit!*

"Mommy! Grandpa and Pop-Pop here," he said, jumping on the bed. He turned to me with a scowl on his face. "Don't kiss my mommy," he said.

"What? Lil nigga, that's my woman and I can kiss her if I want to," I mushed him.

"No, that's my mommy," he said jumping on me.

I laughed and began tickling him. He started laughing uncontrollably and Neicey just shook her head.

"Mykell Sr., we have a problem," my pops said walking into the room.

"What's wrong?" I asked.

He handed me an envelope and I looked back at Neicey, she was looking like she wanted to tear the damn thing open herself. I opened it and read the letter. And my blood started to boil. "What the fuck!" I yelled.

"What?" Neicey asked.

"Tyriq, go play with your brothers," I said.

After he left the room I gave the papers to Neicey. After she read them, she looked from me to pops. “This is a joke right?” she asked.

“I wish, but ain’t no way in hell that bitch getting my son,” I stated.

After two fucking years, Candy’s trifling ass decided she wanted to file for custody of Tyriq and she hasn’t seen him since she left him in that restaurant with me and Neicey. If she thinks she’s getting him, she got another damn thing coming. He doesn’t even remember her ass, he calls Neicey his mother.

“Can she even do that? I mean she hasn’t even seen him in two, almost three years,” Neicey said.

“Don’t worry, she won’t get him,” Pops said.

“Yea baby, don’t even trip, she won’t get him and I promise you that,” I said.

“Yea, but what’s the deal with her requesting a DNA test? If she wasn’t sure he was yours why the hell would she leave him with us?” she asked.

I stopped pacing when I heard her say that, I don’t remember seeing the part about a DNA test, so I was caught off guard. *His ass looks just like me, who else could be the daddy?* I thought, but little did I know, I would soon find out.

“Kell!” I heard Micah yelling from downstairs.

Pops, Neicey and I ran downstairs to see what he was yelling about. When we got down there, Janae was shooting daggers at him and if looks could kill, he probably would have been dead before we even came downstairs.

Micah was pacing just like I was two minutes ago. “Imma kill ya baby mama,” he said.

“Who?” Neicey and I asked.

“Why Pops hand me some papers from Candy talking about she want me to do a DNA test for Tyriq? And if the test comes back that he’s mines she wanna put me on child support,” he fumed.

When he said that, a night that I damn near forgot about came back to my memory, before I could even reminisce, Janae just had to open her mouth.

“That’s nasty, y’all are brothers. How could y’all fuck the same bitch?” she said.

“Well, ain’t that what yo baby daddy and his brother did? Fucked the same bitch?” I questioned, reminding her that she did the same thing, so why is she talking.

“Mykell!” Neicey said cutting her eyes at me.

Jane chuckled. “Say what you really gotta say, Mykell.”

I shrugged, “You don’t have no room to talk because you fucked two brothers and had to do a DNA test so why you speaking on shit?”

"Mykell that's enough, you didn't even have to go there," Neicey said.

"Nah, she should have just stayed in her place and minded her business. Mack, check ya girl," I said, walking back up the stairs leaving everybody standing there.

I went to my bedroom and stripped down to get in the shower. I heard the bedroom door close and I knew it was Neicey. She came into the bathroom. "Can I join you?" she asked.

"Not right now Reneice," I snapped.

She just looked at me like I was crazy before leaving out the bathroom. "Shit," I said to myself. I didn't mean to snap on her like that but I'm tired of the bullshit. Every time I get some damn peace in my life, somebody gotta fuck it up.

I took a quick shower and got out. When I walked back in the room, Neicey was sitting on the bed texting somebody with a smile on her face. When she noticed me coming she put the phone down and got up to take her shower. When she walked past me I grabbed her wrist. "Baby, look..."

"Not right now," she rolled her eyes and snatched her wrist out of my hand.

I just shook my head. "I deserved that," I said.

I went to the dresser to grab myself some boxers when her phone beeped. Since we've been married, we've been checking each other's phones; so I went to see who it was. It was a text from an unknown number.

I really am thankful for you. Like I told you in that letter, I really am sorry for what I did. You could have told Mykell about our little visit and sent him after me but you didn't. I love you, always and forever.

I stood there dumbfounded for a minute because I know I didn't read what I thought I read. I didn't even know her ass was still communicating with him. *What the fuck he mean, their little visit?* I thought as I put the phone down and got dressed.

I didn't even have time to deal with this bullshit.

Reneice

I really didn't have time for Mykell's bullshit today. He's mad because his bitch ass baby mama did some foul shit, so I guess he's going to take it out on everybody else. I've been avoiding him all day. I was in the kitchen with Janae and Lani when I heard Ramone calling my name.

"In the kitchen Daddy-O!" I yelled.

"What the fuck," I heard Lani mumble.

I looked at her to see what was wrong she had a funny look on her face so I followed her eyes. Ramone was standing there with some tall, light skinned chick.

"Ladybug, come here," he said.

"Nah, you come here," I said.

He walked over to me. "Ladybug this is Maya, Maya this is my sister Reneice," he introduced.

It was so quiet you could hear a mouse piss in the floor. She reached her hand out to me and I looked over at Lani then Janae. Lani was pissed and Janae looked like a deer caught in headlights. I walked around her hand and grabbed Ramone by the back of his shirt, pulling him to the basement.

We walked past our dads and the other men and I took him to the office Kell had down there and slammed the door. "Are you fucking serious?!" I yelled.

"What?" he shrugged.

"Ramone Tyshaun Peake, don't fucking play with me because I am two seconds away from slapping the taste out ya fucking mouth."

"Why you tripping? I told you about Maya when you came home," he said.

"I swear I told you I didn't want to meet her ass. Then you bring her to the house knowing Le'Lani is here, and not to mention your fucking kids!" I fumed.

"Reneice calm the fuck down okay. Me and Lani are not together, I can do whatever the fuck I want," he raised his voice.

"Watch who the fuck you talking to," I said.

"Ladybug, I will throw yo pregnant ass out that window, keep playing," he laughed.

I couldn't help but to laugh with him. "Where the hell did she come from anyway? She didn't come down here with you?" I questioned.

"I paid for her flight down here, she just got here."

"I hope yo tricking ass paid for a hotel too because that bitch ain't staying here," I said.

"What?" he laughed.

"I'm serious Ramone, I told you I didn't want to meet her and I can already tell the bitch is stuck up. If I fuck around and slap her ass, it's your fault."

"Just open the door and take ya ass upstairs so you can finish cooking. A nigga hungry."

"Yea, yea, yea." I opened the door and all eyes were on us. I noticed Maya had worked her way downstairs and Lakey was there too.

She walked over to me and Ramone, but I blocked her from getting to him. "You, upstairs. He'll be alright, he's a big boy," I said.

I could feel everybody's eyes on us. I gave her a look that said 'don't play with me' and she headed for the stairs.

"Be nice, Ladybug," my brother whispered in my ear.

I smirked and looked at him with my head tilted. "I'm not promising nothing," I said before heading up the stairs. When I got up the stairs, I found MJ and Chyanne all hugged up. He was whispering something in her ear and she was giggling. I just shook my head at the young love. "MJ, leave that girl alone and go downstairs with your dad and uncles."

"Yea, let me head to the man cave. It's too many women in here for me," he joked.

I hit him the back of the head when he walked passed me and he kissed me on the cheek. I looked around the kitchen and could tell that there was a lot of tension in the room. Chyanne was the only one putting forth the effort to hold a conversation with Maya, only because she didn't know any better. I could tell Lani's mood had changed because she was sitting there nursing a cup of Hennessey and, like me, she wasn't really a drinker.

I walked over to her and looked at her real good. Her eyes were glossy. "How many of them have you had boo?" I asked.

"Since you've been downstairs, she's been chugging em back to back. She's already on her third one," answered Janae.

I took the cup from her and took the bottle off the counter and poured both of them down the drain. I grabbed her hand and led her to the hallway.

"Le'Lani, pull yourself together! This shit is not you; you are never supposed to let a bitch see you sweat. You are a bad bitch in every sense of the word so I need you to act like it. You are letting her think she has the upper hand right now. Fuck Ramone, brother or not."

She nodded her head up and down in agreement, "You're right, mami. Since he wants to play, we can play," she said.

"Exactly! He's the one missing out, not you. You know what to do and you know how to do it." I smiled. "Now let's go," I said, walking back into the kitchen.

"So how far along are you, Chyanne?" Maya asked.

"Five months tomorrow," Chyanne smiled brightly.

"How old are you again?" Maya asked.

Chyanne shifted nervously before she answered, "Sixteen."

"Wow, that's young," she shook her head.

"And? What you trynna say?" Daniella asked.

Everybody's eyes shifted to her because she's usually the quiet one. I stood there, wanting to see how this was going to play out.

"I'm saying that she's too young to be having a baby. She's not even out of high school yet. Sex should be the last thing on her mind," said Maya with her nose in the air.

I noticed Lani tense up, so I gave her a look that said 'not right now' and she fell back. Daniella was cutting up some vegetables but stopped and walked towards Maya.

"Girl, let me tell you something. That girl already has enough people judging her as it is that don't even know her story, so my advice to you is to shut the fuck up if you don't know her situation," she said, waving the knife around in her face.

I looked over at Lani at the same time that she looked at me, then we looked over at Janae and we all smiled. *I knew I liked her for a reason,* I thought as I walked over to Daniella and pulling her back. "Calm down LaLa, I want us to at least eat before you cut her. Let's save the entertainment for later," I giggled.

* * *

Pop-Pop sat at one end of the table while my daddy sat at the other end. The kids had their own table and were in their own little world. I looked around the table and smiled, my family looked good, with the exception of the one who didn't belong here. Everyone was laughing and talking until Chyanne damn near jumped from the table grabbing her stomach.

"What's wrong?" everyone asked simultaneously.

She grabbed MJ's hand and smiled, "He just moved."

Everyone smiled, remembering this was her first child so she wasn't used to this yet. She had a wide smile on her face as she and MJ rubbed all over her stomach.

Daniella playfully whined as she watched the two interact. “Y’all are giving me baby fever,” she joked.

“See, I told you to stay away from her and Neicey, LaLa, I knew they were going to rub off on you. That’s how me and Janae ending up pregnant,” Lani laughed.

“Nah, I wasn’t even around when you found out about Nyla so that one wasn’t my fault,” I joked.

“Yea, hopefully after these two drop, there won’t be no more for a while,” Pop-Pop laughed.

“Shit, I want at least four more,” Ramone said and everyone just looked at him like he was crazy.

“Hell naw! The three you got is enough, I’m too damn young to be a grandpa.” My daddy shook his head.

“Right, you already have *two* princesses and a prince. You good,” I said as I cut my eyes at Lani and got up to get more dressing.

“I’ll be happy to give Ramone a child,” Maya smiled.

I looked over at my brother and he just gulped down the rest of his drink while everyone’s eyes shifted from her to him.

"Maya, no offense but it's time for him to chill out. He has enough as it is and we don't need any more problems."

"Well Neicey..." she started, but I cut her off.

"No, it's Reneice; you only call me Neicey if I give you permission," I said, looking her up and down.

"Reneice, in case you haven't noticed, I'm the lady in your brother's life. He'll never have to worry about a paternity issue with me in his life. I'm not that type of woman. I'll leave that to the rats," she said.

"What the fuck you trynna say?" Lani asked, getting up.

"I think I said what I had to say. That's trashy, you should know how to only sleep with one person at a damn time, then you wouldn't have to worry about who the father of your child is."

"Yo Maya, chill the fuck out," Ramone said, but that wasn't good enough for me. I tried to lunge for that bitch but someway, Mykell grabbed me. It's okay because Lani hit her ass with a good two piece.

Everyone just stood there for a minute because they knew how Lani got if you tried to break up a fight. Finally Ramone grabbed her and drug her up the stairs while she was screaming and yelling. I told his ass not to bring that bitch around but he just had to be hardheaded.

Lani

I tried to fight Ramone off of me the whole time he was dragging me up the stairs. He took me to the room and dropped me on the bed. "Get the fuck out, now!" I yelled.

"One of these days your temper gone get you fucked up," he said calmly.

"Ramone, just get the fuck out my face, I don't have shit to say to you. Go back down there and check on your bitch," I said through gritted teeth.

"I am checking on my bitch. You alright?" he smirked.

"Don't be a smart ass Ramone; I'm not in the mood to play your games."

"Nah, but for real though Le'Lani, I need for you to calm your hot tempered ass down and chill out. All that shit was uncalled for."

I looked at him with my head tilted, ready to slap fire from his ass; instead I just got in my bed and lay down. "I'm too tired to fight and argue with you Ramone, I'm too tired."

Without another word, he left the room. I turned over to my other side so my back was facing the door when I heard the door open again.

"Leave me the hell alone!" I said without looking to see who it was.

"I know you not talking to me, little girl."

I turned around to see my daddy standing there with a smile on his face. In his fifties, Noah Jones was a very handsome man. He had good, curly hair that was cut short without a grey in sight. His goatee was trimmed nice and neat and he was very built for his age. Those hazel eyes that Mykell and Micah inherited from him made him even more handsome than he already was.

"I'm sorry daddy, I thought you were Ramone." I moved over so he could have a seat on the bed.

"I just came in here to talk to you and see what's up; you've been a little distant lately," he said.

"I know daddy but it will get better now, I promise," I sighed.

He looked at me like he knew I was hiding something, "Cut the bullshit Le'Lani, your brother already told me. What I want to know is why you felt like you couldn't come tell me what the fuck was going on?"

I knew he was really pissed for two reasons. One, he only cursed when he was really mad and two, a vein was sticking out on the side of his neck. If you're just meeting my daddy, you would never know or guess that he used to have a very bad temper once upon a time. From what I've been told, it didn't surface until the day I was born, which just so happens to be the day he lost his wife.

"Because daddy, you've been doing good all these years and I refuse for you to have a set back behind me. Also, I did this to myself because I should have listened but I didn't, I got what I deserved, basically," I shrugged.

He got up and started pacing the floor for a few minutes quietly before he decided to speak again. "Le'Lani, you are my daughter, my baby girl, so if somebody is hurting you or disrespecting you, I feel as though they are disrespecting me. That never happens and it's not about to start now. As far as my temper goes, you never get rid of it; you just learn how to deal with it," he said before leaving out of the room.

* * *

I went to check on Zyla and Ranyla to find them both knocked out in the bed with Keiyari. I kissed all of them on the forehead before leaving out the room. When I got back to my room, I ran a bath and put some bubbles in it. I lit a few candles and turned on some music so I could relax.

After getting everything I needed, I got in the tub and laid my head back, letting my sore body soak. Not all of the bruises Zamier put on my body had healed completely, so I was still a little achy on top of my attacking Maya earlier today. I closed my eyes as "Right by My Side" by Nicki Minaj and Chris Brown came on the radio and I sang along.

Gotta let you know how I'm feeling

You own my heart, he just renting

Don't turn away, pay attention

I'm pouring out my heart oh boy

I heard movement by the bathroom door. I opened my eyes to see Ramone standing there. I just stared at him and kept singing.

I, I'm not living life

I'm not living right

I'm not living if you're not by my side

I hadn't even noticed that I was crying until I felt the tears roll down my cheek. Our eyes stayed locked with each other's as he came closer to the tub. He grabbed the rag, poured body wash on it and started washing my back. I flinched a little when he got to the middle of my back because that was still one of my sore spots. Out the corner of my eye I noticed him clench his jaws and he tensed up.

"You deserve way better than this Le'Lani. Any nigga that would put his hands on a female like that is a bitch, hands down."

I didn't respond as he stood me up and finished washing me down, then he let the water out the tub and turned the shower on for me to rinse off. After I was finished, I grabbed the towel and walked into the room so that I could dry off. Ramone just stood in front of me, staring at me the whole time. When I was done, he went into the drawer and got me out some panties and a bra.

"What do you want from me Ramone?" I asked as I put on some shorts and a t-shirt.

"I'm sorry Le'Lani, okay? I know I fucked up and none of this bullshit would be happening if I would have just put my pride aside. That shit really fucked me up though, thinking the child the love of my life carried wasn't mines. Then to find out she's actually mine is some crazy shit."

I chuckled. "Ramone, I accepted Keiyari because he was a part of you and innocent in the whole situation. I have no problems loving him like he's mine, and I even get along with his mother. You kicked me out and turned your back on me because the results didn't say what you wanted them to say. Not only did you turn your back on me, but you also turned your back on that innocent little girl, you also turned your back on Ranyla when you kicked us out the house."

Damn these tears, I thought as I wiped my eyes.

"I know Lani and I regret that shit deeply! All I want is for you...y'all, all three of y'all, to come home. I'm tired of playing these fucking games. I want my family back; it's been too fucking long," he pleaded, not only with his mouth but with his eyes.

"What about the DNA test and what about Maya?" I asked.

He cocked his head to the side and looked at me funny. "Fuck the test; I know that's my daughter. I'm taking y'all back home with me so we can change her last name and put *my* name on her birth certificate."

"Again, what about Maya?" I said slowly.

"Say you'll come home and her ass is a done deal," he said.

I just looked at him, contemplating in my head if I wanted to do this again after all this time and the hurt.

Chapter 10

Ramone

I left Lani at the house with the girls and Keiyari while I went on the hunt. I really hoped that nigga didn't think that I was going to let him live after he put his hands on my girl and daughter. I parked my car down the street from his house and slowly walked to his house. I was dressed in all black and it was night time, so I made sure nobody saw me.

My street instincts kicked in as I picked the lock on the back door. You know what they say, "You can take a nigga out the hood, but you can't take the hood out the nigga." The door unlocked in no time. I took the safety off of my gun before entering.

The house smelled like a damn bar. The alcohol smell was so strong I almost got drunk just from inhaling it. I moved around in the dark, looking for the stairs. When I got upstairs, I looked in all of the rooms until I found the one that my target was sleeping in. It had been some years since I had done this shit, but I have no problems doing it when it came down to my family.

When I reached his bedroom, I flipped on the lights. This nigga was in bed calling hogs. I thought about killing him in his sleep, but I wanted him to know what hit him. I walked over to the bed and hit him in the head with the butt of my gun. He jumped up holding his head.

"Wakey, wakey nigga," I smirked.

He looked lost for a minute but when he realized who I was, he laughed.

"What's funny? I wanna laugh too," I said.

"Nigga, I know good a damn well yo ass not here because of that bitch." He shook his head.

Before I could even respond, he jumped out the bed with a gun that came out of no fuckin where and let off two shots. I felt a burning pain in my shoulder and stomach. I didn't even get a chance to let off a shot before I fell to the ground. He stepped over me smiling.

"My daddy always told me pussy could be a nigga's worst downfall," he laughed, and that was all I remembered before everything went black.

Mykell

I'd been avoiding Neicey's ass like the damn plague for the past week while I finished up some business. I have yet to confront her about the whole Kamil situation, but it was coming and coming soon. I never would have thought the woman I fell in love with would do some sneaky shit behind my back like that, knowing his ass is a damn walking target. It seemed like when it came down to his bitch ass, she could never think straight and made very stupid decisions. I was still trying to figure out why she didn't put a bullet in his ass when she found out about him being part of the plan to kill her ass. I would be lying if I said I didn't feel some type of way about her keeping his ass around. I felt like she had deeper feelings for him than what she let on.

Let me find out and I'll give their asses a double funeral and she can lay right next to him.

On top of all that, Lakey and I had been planning on opening up a club. We only had a little over two weeks until it would be completely finished. We'd been moving in silence about the whole thing, it's supposed to be a surprise to everyone. I was sitting in what was to be my office when Lakey walked in.

"What's up nigga?" I dapped him.

"Shit, just ready for our baby to finally open." He smiled. "What's up with you though? You look like you got a lot on your mind."

"Is it that obvious?" I chuckled.

"Hell yea, talk to me."

"My damn wife, that's it, that's all," I sighed.

"Here y'all go with this shit. Y'all been doing good, so what now?" he asked.

I told him about the text messages I'd seen in her phone, and in return he pulled a folded piece of paper from his wallet and gave it to me. I read it while he told me about MJ coming to him about wanting to kill Kamil. I laughed when I was done reading the letter.

"The shit niggas will do behind some pussy." I shook my head. "No lie, Neicey is working with some killer, so I understand why his ass done lost his mind."

"That nigga is straight tripping. He knew what it was from jump. When he met her, y'all was together. Yea, she ran to his ass when y'all broke up, but she ran right back. I don't know why he thought she would be with him." Lakey shook his head.

"Unless she was making him think she would be with him," I thought out loud.

"C'mon now Kell you don't even believe that shit. You know she wouldn't lead him on with no bullshit like that. One thing I know about Reneice Leila Jones is her ass is *not* going to stay somewhere she doesn't want to be. If she wanted him still, she would be with him and never would have married yo ass."

I slumped in my chair a little thinking about what he had just said. I needed to just go home and talk to her; maybe I was jumping to conclusions and taking shit the wrong way. Then something hit me.

"That's it; we can call the club Leila." I smiled.

Lakey smiled with me and nodded his head, "That's hot."

"Alright man, let me get up out of here and talk to my wife," I said, getting up.

On the way home, they played "Must Be Nice" on the radio and it instantly made me think of when I first met Neicey. She was young and feisty as hell, I laughed at the memory of the first night I met her.

When I got to the house, MJ, Chyanne and Romell were all playing a game while Tyriq played with

Amyricale. I smiled at my kids, and the thought of having another one and possibly a grandchild made me smile even harder. "Where ya mama?" I asked.

"Upstairs," they all answered simultaneously.

I took the stairs two at a time until I reached the bedroom where I heard Neicey singing that damn Ariana Grande song her and Amyricale love so much. She looked up from her laptop when she saw me and looked back down without saying anything. I walked over to the bed, closed her laptop and put it on the dresser.

"We need to talk," I said.

"Then talk."

"So what's up with the text message in your phone I read about Kamil talking about thank you for meeting up with him and not telling me?" I said.

She just looked at me without answering.

"Cat got ya tongue?"

"No, I'm, just waiting for you to answer the question since you usually have all the answers." She shrugged.

"Cut the bullshit Reneice, now is not the time for you to be playing! I'm already going to kill your little boyfriend so you might as well talk!" I yelled.

She got off the bed and laughed. "So is this what it's really about? You're jealous?" she asked.

I looked at her like she had just grown four heads, "What the fuck you just say? What the fuck am I jealous of? I'm the one still hitting the pussy, I got the ring, I got the kids, and you got *my* last name. So what the fuck am I jealous of again?"

She shrugged, "So tell me why you are coming at me on some bullshit then?"

"Because my fucking pregnant ass wife went behind my back to see her no good ass ex that tried to send her ass to fucking prison, dumb ass!" I yelled.

"So I'm dumb? Okay, we'll see who's dumb."

"Yea, ya ass is fucking stupid as fuck, if you wasn't carrying my baby I would be beating yo ass all over this damn room," I said through gritted teeth, even though I didn't mean it.

"How do you know this is your baby?" she sassed and the next thing I knew she was on the ground holding her cheek while MJ pushed me back.

"C'mon now, Pops. Ain't you the one who told me not to ever put my hands on a female? That's your fucking wife, my mother!" he yelled.

Looked over at Chyanne helping Neicey off the floor, I looked back at MJ. "Nah MJ, she fucking killed your mother a while back and if she keep fucking with me, Imma send her ass to be with her," I said.

Neicey laughed, "You ain't shit."

"I guess that makes two of us," I smirked.

Neicey's phone rung and she answered it. "Yes, daddy?" she answered.

Whatever Big Mone just said made Neicey turn pale white and she dropped her phone. MJ grabbed the phone while I grabbed Neicey. She started shaking and let out a wail that I had never heard before.

"What's wrong baby?" I asked.

It's funny how not even two minutes ago I slapped the shit out of her, now I'm concerned about her.

"My…My brother. Zamier shot my brother," she cried.

Reneice

Even though Pop-Pop sent his private jet to come get us, it seemed like it took us forever to get back to Detroit. As soon as we got to the hospital, I jumped out of the car before Mykell could even come to a complete stop. I ran into the waiting room to find everyone sitting around.

"What happened daddy? Any news?" I asked my dad when I got to him.

He shook his head. "All I know is he was shot in the shoulder and stomach."

I swear it felt like all the wind was knocked out of me. I couldn't lose my brother. He had raised me, been by my side no matter what, had my back through thick and thin. Yea, we may fight and argue, but what siblings don't? This shit couldn't be happening.

I looked to see Maya walking into the waiting room. I immediately jumped up in her face. "Why are you here?"

"I called her," a nurse answered for her.

"What the fuck for? This is a family matter, her ass has no right to be here and I know damn well she's not listed as an emergency contact."

"Because that is my cousin's boyfriend laying in there fighting for his life, she has the right to know," the nurse said, trying to get loud.

I laughed at these two dumb bitches. "Boyfriend? In case you haven't noticed bitch, Ramone moved Le'Lani and his *daughters* back into *their* house. Now you got two seconds to walk the fuck back out that door before I show my ass because if you thought Le'Lani fucked you up, you ain't ready to see me," I said as calmly as possible.

"I don't have to go anywhere, I have just as much of a right to be here as she does," Maya opposed.

"Bitch I'll---" I started, but was cut off by Mykell whispering in my ear.

"Just calm the fuck down, let her ass stay here, you can't kick her out of a damn public hospital."

I rolled my eyes and walked away from them. "I don't have time for this bullshit! My fucking brother is fighting for his damn life," I said out loud

I just wanted to get away from everybody, I was already pissed before we got this fucked up news and it didn't make the situation any better. I zipped up my coat and went outside for some fresh air. I know they'll come get me if the doctor comes out.

I found a bench and just sat there thinking. My life had been crazy since the day I lost my mom. They say life has its ups and downs, but to me it seemed like the downs were winning by a long shot. I shook my head at the thought of Mykell having the nerve to slap me over some bullshit. Yea, it's not the first time he's done it, but it'd been years. I know I was wrong for even insinuating this baby could be Kamil's but I just wanted him to feel what I was feeling; hurt.

I was brought out of my thoughts by a pair of arms wrapping around me and someone else sitting next to me. "Is this cold air good for the baby?" Daniella smiled.

I smiled faintly and looked over at Lakey. I looked from him to her again and smiled. "You guys are a beautiful couple, I'm very happy that my knucklehead found you. He's very happy," I said to her.

"Telling all my business, huh?" he laughed.

"No I'm serious. You know we've known each other all our lives so I can tell when you are genuinely happy, and plus it's written all over your face. Just treat her right and don't let her go, or I'll have to kill you."

"How you threatening me?" he shook his head.

"I'm just playing…No, I'm not." We all laughed.

"See mama, that's all you needed; a good laugh," Daniella smiled.

"You're right LaLa, it's so much crazy shit going on."

"I know, but you have to remember stress is not good for you or the baby."

"I know," I sighed.

We heard footsteps coming and we all turned our heads at the same time. "The doctor is ready," my daddy said and we all jumped up. We walked swiftly into the waiting room to hear what the doctor has to say.

"Alright Doc, we're ready."

"Mr. Peake took a bullet to the abdomen and the shoulder. We got the bullet out of his shoulder with no problems but the one in his stomach was a little stubborn. The good thing is it didn't hit any major arteries so he'll be fine," the doctor said, and I felt a big weight lift off my shoulders.

"Can we see him?" Lani asked.

"We gave him some very heavy sedatives so he'll be out of it for the night, but you can come back in the morning."

"Thank you soooo much," I said to the doctor.

After leaving the hospital, we all headed to our destinations. I guess Pop-Pop could tell there was something going on between me and his son because he kept looking at us funny. He decided not to speak on it though…for now at least.

* * *

The next morning I woke up with an attitude for some reason. My baby was in a damn good mood today so she was kicking, and kicking hard, and it was aggravating me. Everyone was walking around with smiles like my brother wasn't laying up in the damn hospital.

"See Lani, I told you to not to mess with that nigga." Mykell shook his head.

"How was I supposed to know he was crazy?" she laughed.

"I really don't find it funny that my brother is in the hospital because of that nigga, all behind you though," I said.

Everyone just stopped and looked at me. "What are you saying, Neicey?" Micah asked.

"I think I said it. If she would have left him alone the first time he went upside her head like Mykell told her to, we wouldn't even be going through this shit."

"This shit ain't my fault Reneice," Lani said getting up.

“How the hell is it not? You acted so fucking simple knowing if his ass hit you once, he was going to do it again. So why the fuck would you stay with him? Especially after he told you about the damn DNA test?” I said through gritted teeth.

She looked at Mykell. “Really, Kell? You been discussing my business?” she asked.

“Man, Le’Lani gone with all that, that’s my wife.” He waved her off.

“That don’t mean shit! You just told us you had to slap some sense into her ass, so you wasn’t worried about her being your wife then.”

“I honestly think you better back the fuck away from me Le’Lani and I’m not even playing with you right now. You think just because we got into a little fight that he’s not my husband anymore? We said until death do us part. You know, you were this close to being somebody’s wife, until you had to fuck it up.” I rolled my eyes.

“Y’all seriously need to chill, ‘y’all are fucking sisters,” Micah said.

“Neicey, keep running ya mouth and I’ll beat ya pregnant ass. You need to be worried about how long you’ll be able to keep your fucking *husband,*” she laughed.

I jumped up. “I don’t take kindly to threats, pregnant or not, this is not what you want baby girl, and you fucking know it.”

Mykell got in between us and pushed his sister back a little. “Le’Lani, you’re my sister and I love you, but don’t roll up on her like that; especially while she’s carrying my seed,” he said.

“Fuck that bitch.”

“Don’t fuck me, fuck with me,” I said.

“Alright, that fucking enough. Everybody sit the fuck down, now!” Pop-Pop yelled while coming down the stairs.

“No disrespect Pop-Pop, but I have better things to do than to sit here,” I said, getting up and walking towards the door.

I walked outside to my car and jumped in, Mykell stood there trying to get in but I kept shaking my head no. I put the car in reverse and sped off. I reached for my phone and powered it off, knowing he was about to blow my phone up. I took the two hour drive to the only place I knew I could find peace.

When I pulled up to the cemetery, I felt a sense of calm come over me. I had stopped by the store and got me some flowers to put on my mommy’s grave. I haven’t been here to visit her since before I left for college, and that was years ago. I sat my big pregnant ass on the ground in front of her headstone, not caring about it being cold out.

“Hey mommy,” I smiled. “I know it’s been a long time since I’ve came to see you and I’m sorry. It’s been so much going on that I haven’t been focusing on the most important things or the things that matter.”

I wiped the tears away that had snuck and fell before continuing.

"Mommy, I need you. I've tried to be as strong as I could, but I'm tired. I'm tired mommy. I know you didn't raise me to be weak but I…I guess I'm just tired. I'm always there for other people and I'm always strong for everybody else but I need somebody to be strong for me." I sighed as I got up and kissed her headstone.

"I love you mommy, I promise I'll come back soon."

I got back in my car, contemplating if I wanted to go back to Pop-Pop's house or take that long drive back to Florida. I knew I wouldn't hear the last of it if I didn't go see my brother so I decided to do that then stay at my daddy's house.

Chapter 11

Janae

I sat there with the test results in my hand. I wanted to look at them but then again I was scared, because a very little part of me has a doubt. I don't want to feel like I let Rodney down but I guess I did that the moment I became intimate with his brother. I waited for Micah to get in the house before I opened the envelope.

As soon as Micah walked through the door, I dragged him upstairs.

"Damn baby, I know you're happy to see me but damn," he laughed.

I smacked my lips, "Shut up." I held the package out for him. "Here."

He looked down at it then back at me. "What it say?"

"I don't know, I was waiting for you to look then tell me," I said.

He took the package and opened the envelope before reading it over. He peeked at me over the top of the papers then went back to reading. Finally, he looked back at me and smiled. "Bishop is not the father."

"I knew it!" I said, releasing a breath I didn't even realize I was holding. I ran to the dresser and grabbed my cell phone off the charger while I immediately dialed Bishop's number.

"Yea," he said, unenthused.

"I take it you got the mail and the results," I said.

"Yea, I told you all I wanted was the truth and now I got it, so you don't have to worry about that anymore but I would at least like to get to know my only niece. I think my brother would have liked that."

"Look Bishop, I don't have a problem with you getting to know your niece. I would love for you to get to know her, I just don't want no bullshit," I said seriously.

"C'mon Nae Nae, chill with all that," he chuckled.

"I'm not playing with you Bishop."

"I know you're not."

"Cool, I call you with some arrangements then."

"That will be cool."

I hung up the phone and looked at Micah. "I guess you're next," I said.

"Like hell. I'm not taking no damn DNA test," he said, looking at me like I'm crazy.

"Why not, Micah? You slept with her, didn't you?" I asked, matching his attitude.

"Janae, don't even try it, you just want me to admit to the bullshit but I'm not even about to go there with you right now," he said.

"She wouldn't be requesting a DNA test for her son if you didn't sleep with her."

He stopped and rubbed down his face with his hand before speaking again, "Alright," he shrugged. "Me and Kell ran a train on the bitch, but that was way before I met you and back when Neicey was in a coma. It happened one time and one time only, so therefore I know for a fact that Tyriq is my *nephew* and not my *son*. I will still go to court to support my little brother but all that other bullshit ain't happening."

I was stuck for a minute because I couldn't believe he would actually admit to it but I can't even be mad because the shit happened. I trust him and I know he would never cheat on me or do anything to hurt me.

"It's crazy how after all the shit that Mykell and Neicey have been through they still manage to be happy," I said as I sat on the bed.

"They literally have been through hell and back, but no matter what always seem to get it together," said Micah, walking out of the closet.

"Yea, I just hate that after all this time her and Lani got into it. I would hate for their friendship to end." I shook my head.

"Don't even trip, emotions were high that night and they both are one and the same and speak whatever comes to their mind, which is why they were made to be friends. They'll eventually get it together, they're both being stubborn right now. Plus, Pops and Big Mone not about to let that shit slide," he laughed.

"I really thought they were about to fight though."

"They probably would have, but let another bitch say something to one of them today, I bet you they will forget they were ever beefing and beat that bitch ass like it's nothing." He smiled, jumping on the bed with me.

"Mack, can I ask you a question?" I looked at him so he would know that I was serious.

"Yea, what's up?"

I sat there thinking of a way to word what I wanted to ask him. I couldn't find the right words so I just right on out and said it. "Do you think I'm a bird bitch because I slept with Bishop? I mean do you look at me differently now?" I asked.

He sat up on the bed. "Janae look, I really don't give a fuck what you did in your past. That shit was before me and nobody is perfect, that's including me. I don't look at you any differently than I did the first time I laid eyes on you. The only reason I was mad was because you kept it from me and I thought you were still fucking that nigga because you had him in my house."

"I just don't want you to think that I would try to do something with Mykell, or even Ramone, for that matter. I was young and I made a big mistake that I'm still regretting to this day."

"Oh, I know you wouldn't do that. Even if you did, I'm not the one you would have to worry about because Neicey and Le'Lani would slaughter yo ass if you even tried." He laughed and I just punched him in the arm playfully.

"Whatever Micah," I laughed with him.

Lani

"I'm telling you Ramone, she bucked like she really wanted to fight," I explained what happened to him what happened between me and his sister.

"Lani, you should have not even said nothing to her, you know how her ass gets when she got a lot going on. Ladybug wasn't built to handle stressful situations like that and shit," he said.

I looked at him like I wanted to slap the shit out of him in that damn hospital bed. "I should have known you would take up for her." I rolled my eyes.

"You damn right. Just like I took up for you when I said she was wrong for blaming the shit on you. I'm not taking nobody's side because I refuse to get in the middle of it. Knowing y'all, you gon be back the best of friends before the end of the week," he said while throwing a piece of ice at my head.

"Yea, okay, she step to me like that again and I will have no choice but to beat her lil pregnant ass," I chuckled.

"You ain't gon do shit or I'll have to fuck you up myself. You better leave my Ladybug alone."

"Shut up…By the way, Carmen text me and said she'll be bringing the kids back in another hour, the girls don't want to leave Keiyari."

"They miss their brother." He gave me the side eye.

"Don't go there Ramone, I thought..." I stopped mid-sentence when I saw Maya walk into the room. I rolled my eyes over to Ramone and he looked annoyed.

"I hope I'm not interrupting," she said sarcastically.

"Actually you are, we were actually having family time. Ramone, I thought you gave her ass her walking papers," I said, never taking my eyes off her.

"Chill Lani," he said.

"Yea, chill Lani, I don't know why you feel so threatened by me," she smiled.

"Bitch, don't nobody have to be threatened by your ass, you're a fucking nobody. I already told your ass once, which was one too many times for me, so it would be in your best interest for me not to make me say it again. Disappear on your own bitch or I'll make it happen for you," we all heard someone say.

Everybody's eyes shifted to the door where Neicey was standing with Big Mone by her side. She was glaring a hole through Maya and I wanted to laugh because Maya actually looked frightened by Neicey's threat, which I knew for a fact that she would make good on if she had to.

Big Mone whispered something in her ear and she put on a fake smile while walking towards Ramone's hospital bed.

"Anyways Ramone, I just came to see how you were doing. I'll talk to you later," said Maya, moving towards the door.

"I highly doubt that, lose the number," Neicey said.

Big Mone came over to me and gave me a hug and a kiss on the cheek. "How's my favorite daughter-in-law?" he asked.

"I'm good, but I'm not too sure that I'm your daughter-in-law since I don't have a ring or anything," I said, cutting my eyes at Neicey while she rolled her eyes at me in response.

"Alright, now that I have both of you here in the same room, it's time we cut the bullshit. I don' like the shit I heard about you two thinking it was okay for y'all to talk crazy to each other and think y'all were about to go to blows. I don't care who said what or who did what, but it's done, over with and y'all are over it. I don't want no more shit out of either of you," Ramone said, looking from his sister to me.

She was playing on her phone acting like she didn't hear shit he said and I just shook my head. *This girl is so damn stubborn.*

He pinched her in her arm and she winced in pain. "Oooouch! Why you do that? Daddy!" she whined.

"You should really listen to your brother; he knows what he's talking about," Big Mone laughed.

"I heard him but he didn't have to pinch me," she mumbled.

Being the bigger person, I decided to start up a conversation with her. "So when do you go to the doctors to find out what you're having?"

"In two days," she answered.

"Wait, Mykell goes to court tomorrow though," I said.

"I know, and I leave tonight."

"So you're not going?" I asked as if I didn't believe her.

"Nah, I have to get back and check on Chyanne because she wasn't feeling too good before we left and I'm also taking her to her appointment. But no worries, he has you guys to be there for him and show support. Besides, I don't want to have to choke his baby mama."

I laughed, those two are always fighting like damn cats and dog but knowing damn well they're not going anywhere.

Mykell

I was speeding down the street, hoping I wouldn't be late. This was a very important appointment that I refused to miss. When I got to my destination, I rushed to the front desk and got the information I needed. When I reached the door, I took a deep breath before opening the door. *I made it just in time.* Chyanne was sitting in the chair and Neicey was lying on the table. She looked confused when she noticed me walk through the door.

"What are you doing here?" she asked.

"I came to check on you and my daughter," I looked over at Chyanne. "And grandson."

"Too bad you're having a granddaughter," Chyanne laughed.

"Aw shit, I guess there won't be a Mykell the Third, huh?"

"Again, what are you doing here?" Neicey questioned again.

"Court was cancelled because nobody can find Candy and I got the test done on Tyriq before we even left for Detroit and it confirmed what I already knew; he's mine," I answered.

Thirty minutes later, we were walking out of the doctor's office anticipating the arrival of our new princess, Kamora Cherice Jones. Only two more months to go and she'll be here. I decided to take the ladies shopping so they could get some stuff for the new additions to the family. I don't care what anyone says or what the results come out to be, Chyanne and that baby will always be a part of our family, and I'm pretty sure everyone else feels the same way.

"So Chy Chy, what are we naming the baby?" I asked.

"Since it's a girl, she will be Mikyah Jadore Jones."

"That's cute!" Neicey gushed.

"Yea, I like that," I agreed.

We were walking through the mall when someone bumped into Chyanne, and just my damn luck, it was none other than the infamous Toni Hunt. *Lord please be with me.* "Just keep walking and don't say nothing." I told Neicey.

"Really Mykell? That's how you act after all the business we handled?" Toni smiled and I knew right then this bitch was really delusional.

I kept walking hoping Neicey would do the same and not act a damn fool, my prayers were answered because she just chuckled and walked away.

"It's okay Mykell, this won't be the last time you see me," she laughed.

After we left the mall, we headed straight for the house because Neicey's feet were swollen and hurting and Chyanne's back was hurting. Dealing with two pregnant women at one time almost drove me crazy. When we got to the house, Neicey went straight for the stairs to lie down while I waited for MJ to come back with his brothers and sister.

Tired of playing the waiting game, I went upstairs to find Neicey standing in the full body mirror looking over herself. She kept rubbing her hands over the little scar from the bullet wound where she got shot. I walked up behind her, rubbing her stomach and she just stared at me through the mirror.

"Baby, I'm sorry, I should have never put my hands on you but I let my anger get the best of me when you tried to say this wasn't my daughter, and even though I know you were just trying to hurt me, you didn't deserve to be hit." I kissed her neck. She didn't say anything but kept staring at me, I don't know why but for some reason I felt like I was losing her.

"All I want to know is, do you have feelings for that nigga?" I asked.

She nodded her head, "Of course I *had* feelings for him. If I didn't I would have never brought him around my kids or my family."

"Okay, but why didn't you cut him off when you found out about him being hired to kill you and when he shot you?"

"I did," she said.

"But then you let him come back in. You kept him around."

"Did I not keep *you* around and let *you* come back in when you cheated on me with Kya?"

"That's different though, Reneice and you know it," I protested.

"How so? Both of you did some shit to me to hurt me, but I forgave both of y'all and let you stay in my life, and in his defense he didn't mean to shoot me. That bullet was meant for you," she said while walking away.

I felt myself getting angry. "So now you're going to take up for the nigga?"

She shook her head and rolled her eyes at me. "Really Mykell? Just ask me what you really want to ask me and stop beating around the damn bush! You want to know if I love him and if I want to be with him? I have love for him but I'm far from being in love with him. I'm in love with you! I married you! I'm where I want to be, Mykell. If I wanted to be with him, I would have never got back with you," she yelled.

"Alright, I believe you," I simply said.

"You don't have a damn choice." She lay on the bed.

I sat on the end of the bed and took her right foot into my hand and started rubbing it. It was swollen as fuck, I felt sorry for her because they didn't even look normal.

"Baby, you know how a while back I said we should go see a marriage counselor?" I asked.

"Mykell, unless you're thinking about divorcing me, I am not going to no damn marriage counselor," she said, giving me the evil eye.

"Alright but let me ask you this...Do you trust me?"

She looked at me for a minute before speaking. "It's getting better. Well, it was until you started staying out longer than you need to, but even with that, my woman's intuition isn't telling me that you're having an affair," she answered honestly.

"Why did you marry me if you don't trust me?" I wanted to know what's going on in her head and in her heart. She hates talking to me about her problems because she would rather run.

"I said I didn't trust you, as in once upon a time, and honestly, because I'm used to being hurt by the people I trust." She shrugged.

"What you mean? Care to elaborate?" I asked, moving to my left foot.

"It's like this, since I was eleven years old, I have been getting hurt by people I love and trust. My mommy died and left me when I was 11, my brother got locked up when I needed him the most, I didn't meet my daddy until I was twenty years old because I thought he was a deadbeat, I found out somebody I trusted and confided in was in on a plan to kill me and tried to send my husband away for life, and you, you cheated on me when all I wanted was to be loved and be happy for once," she said, wiping her tears away.

I just sat there dumbfounded for a moment because I never looked at it like that. Then on top of all that, she was raped twice, shot, beaten, and had a miscarriage. Now I realize that all she wanted from me was to love her and make her a happy woman and my dumb ass fucked all that up in the beginning.

“Are you happy now? I mean with me?”

She laughed, “Mykell how many times do I have to tell you that I’m where I want to be? If I wasn’t happy, you know I would not still be here. Yes, we have fights and arguments, but please tell me what one relationship doesn’t?”

“I love you.”

“You better,” she joked.

Chapter 12

MJ

For some reason today, Chyanne had been avoiding me. When she saw me coming down the hall, she would hurry up and walk the other way. I sent her five texts and she wouldn't return any of them. When lunch time came around, I went looking for her, only to find her in the hallway with DeAndre; her ex and my number one enemy. They didn't see me coming, but I could hear what they were talking about as I got closer.

"I don't know why you still mess with his little ass Chy baby. I told you Vanessa was talking about how he came to see her Saturday and you know how she get down."

"Okay, what do you want me to do? I'm pregnant as hell so I can't beat her ass like I want to, plus I don't even think me and him are together anyways; so he can do what he wanna do." She shrugged.

"Fuck that nigga, you just making excuses to justify what he did. Ain't that why you broke up with me? You know that's supposed to be my baby you carrying," he said, touching her stomach.

"Bitch, you better move yo hand off my girl and my daughter," I said, making my presence known.

"What are you doing out here, MJ?" Chyanne asked.

"What the hell you think? I know you seen me texting you so don't play," I was talking to her but my eyes never left DeAndre.

"Ay lil dude, grown folks are out here trying to have a conversation. You should learn how to stay in a child's place."

"What nigga?" I said, walking up on him, only for Chyanne to grab my arm and pull me back.

"Dre leave him the hell alone, you always want to start some shit. Let's go MJ."

"Whatever Chyanne, you know where home at, so I'm not worried. You were mines for two years before you started playing with little boys. You know I don't have a problem playing daddy." He laughed.

And that's when I snapped. I pulled my arm out of Chyanne's grasp and went to him. I punched that bitch right in his jaw and kept following up with blows. I blacked out and fucked his shit up until I heard Chyanne let out a scream that I had never heard before. I snapped out of it and looked at her to see her holding her stomach with her jeans getting soaked with blood. I fucking panicked.

The next thing I knew, I was driving behind the ambulance while on the phone with my dad. "Dad, it was so much blood. She's six months pregnant and I don't know what I would do if she loses my daughter." I wiped my tears away.

"Calm down MJ, don't think the worst. Everything will be alright, that baby is a Jones so you know she's a fighter, her and Chyanne."

"I know, I just feel like shit," I said, pulling into the hospital and throwing my car in park.

"We're five minutes from the hospital. I'll see you when we get there," my dad said before hanging up.

I tried to go back there with Chyanne but they wouldn't let me. I paced the floor back and forth so fast it was making me dizzy. A few minutes later, my dad came running through the doors while my mom waddled. I looked up at her and kind of laughed to myself because she was as big as a house and walking like a penguin.

"Don't be laughing at me, boy." She hit my arm. "Now what's going on and why I get a call talking about you're suspended for fighting? Never mind, that's not important right now."

"I think I fucked up Ma, I really do," I said trying not to break down.

I usually don't cry, not even when I found out that my birth mother was dead. Hell, the bitch never did anything for me anyway. She was a fucking crack head that put niggas before me. But this shit had me ready to have a damn nervous breakdown.

My mom took me into her arms and rubbed my back. "It's not your fault Mykell Jr. Do you hear me? None of this is your fault. We're not sure what happened with Chyanne, but I don't want you blaming yourself."

See, this is exactly why I'm happy my dad decided to get it together and marry my mom. She's so gentle, loving and caring. I'm not sure that he would have found anybody else as perfect as her. She knows what to say, when to say it and how to say it.

We sat there for over an hour before the doctor final came out. By that time, Uncle Lakey and LaLa showed up.

"Family of Chyanne Williams," he announced.

I was the first one to jump up. "How's my girl and daughter, sir?" I asked.

"Well, son, Ms. Williams is a little tired and sore. She had a tear in her uterus which was the cause for the bleeding. We had to take the baby right away if we wanted her to have a chance for survival. She weighs 2lbs even and she's currently in the NICU."

"So she could make it? Being premature and everything? Can I see her?" I asked.

"I have no doubts that she could make it but she would have to stay here until she is healthy enough to come home. I'm pretty sure you know there are a lot of complications that can come with being a premature baby. But we'll discuss that later, let's go see your daughter."

He took me to this room where I had to wash my hands and put on scrubs. She was in this tube looking bed and had lots of tubes coming out of her. I wanted to touch her but I didn't want to hurt her because she was so little. She was about the size of my hand.

"Hey Mikyah, it's daddy. I know you're a fighter, baby girl, so just be strong for me and your mommy. I know we kept saying we were excited to meet you but I didn't expect for you to come early," I slightly chuckled. "You have to get better so you can come home. Your nana and papa are already talking about spoiling you. Oh, and MyMy was already calling you her baby so you have to get better so your auntie can see you." I watched as her little chest slightly moved up and down. I was starting to get emotional and wanted to cry again. "I love you princess and I'll be here to see you every day after school. I guess you were an early birthday present huh? Well, you're the best present I could ever ask for." I smiled at her one more time before blowing her a kiss and leaving the room.

Chyanne

"I failed her already, Mama. I couldn't even do the right thing and let my baby be born healthy," I cried.

Mama Neicey came over to my bed and rubbed my hand while leaning down to kiss my cheek. I felt like shit. I had failed my daughter already. I'm not fit to be anybody's mother. Hell, I should have known that because my own mother wasn't a fit mother.

"Chyanne look at me, you did not fail her. I'm going to tell you like I told MJ, none of this is your fault, alright? Your body had a mind of its own and you could not control what was going on. That baby is going to be alright and in a couple of months we will be taking her home." She smiled at me.

MJ came into the room and I broke down all over again. “I’m sorry, MJ, I’m so sorry,” I cried.

Mama Neicey moved away so MJ could come by the bed. He leaned down and hugged me tightly. “You don’t have to be sorry Chy Chy. Our princess is here and breathing and that’s all that matters. We have to be strong for each other in order for us to be strong for her. She’ll make it, so don’t even worry yourself about all that.”

“Yea, my granddaughter will be perfectly fine. We’ll be here every day to check on her and see her,” Daddy Kell said.

“Her Uncle Lakey and Auntie LaLa will be coming by to see her too, that’s without a doubt,” Uncle Lakey said.

MJ and I wiped my tears away. “I don’t know what I would do without you guys. You are honestly more family to me than my own blood. The school called my mom and told her what happened, but she told them I wasn’t her problem anymore. But it’s okay because I don’t need her as long as I have you all.”

“That’s right. Fuck them, they’ll be the ones missing out on that precious baby’s life,” Uncle Lakey said.

“I just want to thank you for accepting me and bringing me into the family.” I smiled.

“Girl stop, you are family. MJ made that very clear the first day he brought you home, so who are we to argue with that?” Mama Neicey laughed.

I looked around, noticing how blessed I truly was. Even though my own mother and father didn't want anything to do with me, I still had this wonderful family that has been by my side since I met them. Things ain't all good, but they're definitely not all bad.

Chapter 13

Reneice

It's a Friday night and instead of having my pregnant ass in the house eating a quart of cookies and cream ice cream, Mykell had me sitting in the car while he drove around the damn city with a blindfold over my eyes. At first I thought it was cute, but then I started to get nervous.

"Mykell, are you sure that you're not trying to take me to a secret hiding place and kill me?" I half joked.

"Baby just calm down, please? I am not going to kill you, I have a surprise for you. So just sit back, relax and enjoy the ride."

He came home around 9:00 with a suit on, looking very delicious and told me to get dressed. He had this very elegant black dress that was very beautiful with some silver flats to accommodate my swollen feet. I didn't ask any questions and just did as he asked me to.

Finally, the car stopped and I could hear lots of voices. I heard the car door open and close before the passenger's side door opened and he grabbed my hand, telling me to get out. I grabbed his hand and stepped out of the car. He stood behind me with his hands on the blindfold. When he took it off, my jaw hit the ground.

In big bright lights was the word 'Leila's' and it took me a minute to register the fact that my middle name was on a building. I turned around and looked at

Mykell. He was smiling very proudly then starting laughing.

"Close ya mouth before a bug fly in it, baby."

"Mykell what...how...when?" I couldn't even get out a full question.

"Baby, you are looking at the co-owner of Leila's," he smiled.

"Well, who is the other owner?" I asked.

"That would be me," I heard from behind me. I turned around to find Lakey standing there in a suit also with LaLa on his arm.

"Lashaun Marlon Mitchell, why the hell didn't you tell me?" I asked Lakey, calling him by his government name.

"Because it was a surprise, Snook," he laughed.

"Are we going to stand out here all night, or are we going in?" Mykell asked.

"Shut up and let's go." I smiled as the men escorted us into the building. There were people everywhere. Mykell pulled me through a private door that led to a little hallway which eventually led to the elevator. There were two floors to the club, then his and Lakey's offices were on the third floor. We got off on the third floor where there was a big glass window so that you could see over the club. There were two big doors that said 'Mykell' and 'Lakey'. The other couple headed to Lakey's office, while Mykell opened the door to his for us.

I was in awe, it was very spacious. He had big pictures of me, Lani, Amyricale, and even an old picture of his mother when she was young. They were all in black and white and spread out on different walls in his office.

"This is beautiful," I said.

"Yea, I had to put up the faces of the most important ladies in my life," he smiled.

He walked in front of me and looked me up and down. He stood there just staring at me like he had lost his damn mind. "What?" I asked.

"You know, I was just thinking…we should properly bless this office," he said, unbuttoning the jacket to his suit.

"You can't be serious right now Mykell, there's a lot of people down there and aren't you supposed to be down there mingling with the people?" I asked, only for it to fall on deaf ears.

"What? Girl hush. We got managers and shit to make sure everything runs smoothly. The only thing you need to be worried about is getting out that damn dress," he said, licking his lips.

"Nooo Mykell, I don't even have any extra clothes."

He grabbed me and turned me around so he could unzip my dress, then he sat me on top of his desk. “You know I hate when you don’t listen, and I hate it even more when you tell me no.” He kissed my neck all the way down to my stomach. “Don’t be hardheaded like your mommy, baby girl,” he whispered to my stomach.

Then he walked over to the door and locked it before coming back to me. Once again he just stood there staring at me, and it was making me self-conscious. “You are fucking perfect. How did I end up so lucky to have you?” he asked.

I blushed. This is the Mykell I fell in love with, the thug with a passionate side. He leaned down and kissed so passionately it took my breath away. In the middle of the kiss, I felt his hardness enter me and I hadn’t even notice him unbutton his pants. All I could do was gasp. “Mykell,” I moaned.

“See what happens when you tell me no?” he pumped in and out of me. “All I wanted was a little quickie from my wife. Was that too much to ask for?” He talked shit as he hit my spot like he was trying to prove a point.

“Ahhh!” I cried out. “Right there baby,” I moaned.

“Oh you mean right here?” He pumped faster as I felt my juices rain down.

“Yesss!”

“Ughh,” he grunted as he kissed my neck. “That’s what I’m talking about.” He smiled.

I laughed while pushing him away from me. “You play too much for me.”

“Yea whatever, you like it though.”

“No, I don’t, and didn’t nobody tell yo black ass to bust in me either.” I playfully rolled my eyes.

“Shut up, it ain’t like I can get you pregnant while you are already pregnant.” He laughed while heading to the bathroom in his office. I got up and followed him.

“How did you sneak this past me?” I asked.

“You remember when I used to go to ‘handle some business’? Well this is what I was doing, me and Lakey.”

After washing up, we got dressed in some extra clothes that he had brought with him earlier that day, we headed to the dance floor where we met up with Lakey and Daniella. The four of us made the best out of the guys’ grand opening. I was proud of my husband and his legit business.

Big Mone

Noah and I sat outside Zamier’s house for an hour staking it out. This nigga was bold as hell. He wasn’t even trying to lay low, knowing he shot my son. And what makes it so bad, his ass had the nerve to come back to the exact house he shot him in.

Both Noah and I have a personal vendetta against this little nigga since he likes to beat on women and is trigger happy. After playing the waiting game and figuring he wasn't planning on leaving the house anytime soon, we decided to go in. We used the back door and crept in the house. We followed the sound of the TV to the living room, where he was sprawled out on the couch.

I took out my gun and made sure the silencer was screwed on before shooting his bitch ass in the knee. "AHHHH! FUCK!" he yelled like the little bitch he was.

"Move if you want to and I'll blow yo fucking head off," Noah threatened.

I had a rush of excitement come over me because the last time I did this, I ended up in prison. This time, I vowed that I would walk away scot-free and without a trace.

"What the fuck y'all want man? Damn!" he yelled, out holding his knee.

We looked at each other giving each other the signal before empting our clips into his body. See, that was my son's fault when he came to do this the first time. He did too much talking. If you come to do a job, then get it done. There ain't no need to be talking about the shit.

We left out just as quietly as we came in. When we got down the block from his house, Noah placed a call to the Silent Observer, our local Crime Stoppers

Program, and left a tip of a break in. “All our troubles are over.” I smiled.

“Hell yea, now the only thing we have to worry about is getting down to Florida to see about our great granddaughter,” Noah said.

“Yea, we’ll take that trip real soon.

The next morning, I woke up to the sound of my phone ringing.

“Hello?” I answered.

“You did it didn’t you?” Ramone asked.

“Did what, nigga?” I played dumb.

“You know what old man, it’s all on the news.”

“Maybe I did…maybe I didn’t.” I smiled.

“Oh I know you did. Even though I would have loved to do it myself, I appreciate it.”

“Boy stop, I took care of the problem like I told you I would. Tell Lani to sleep easy.”

“I will, old man,” he said before hanging up.

I laid back down thinking about how I might want to move down south with Ladybug and Mykell. The Sunshine State has been calling my name for months, and it’s time I answered.

Chapter 14

Four months later

Chyanne

One hundred and twenty-one days later, totaling up to four months, and today is the day I get to take my precious baby girl home. It's been a long journey, but she made it. My baby is now 7lbs 6oz and the only complications she could have is asthma. Everything has been looking up for me. I've been working at LaLa's boutique, my grades are excellent, MJ and I have been getting along perfectly, and I even saved up enough money to buy me a little car, nothing fancy though.

I pulled up to the hospital and was shocked that MJ had beaten me here. I walked into the nursery to find MJ, Dad, Mom and Grandpa Mone there waiting.

I hugged everybody and gave baby Kamora a kiss on the cheek. "I'm so excited," I gushed.

"We all are. See, I told you that you had nothing to worry about. I knew my baby would be a fighter. My little Mikyah Jadore." Mama smiled.

"I can see it now, her and Kamora are going to be wreaking havoc together and I can't forget about Amyricale. She'll be the ring leader," MJ laughed.

We all laughed because we knew it was the truth. Amyricale was something else at three years old, I swear that little girl been here before. The nurse brought out Mikyah and I got so happy. Holding her right now is more joyous than it was when I held her for the first time, only because I know she gets to go home with me today.

She looked up at me and smiled like she knew what was going on and I smiled back at her.

"MJ go over there and stand by Chyanne so I can take a picture," Dad said.

The three of us took a family picture then we did the necessary paper work so we could take our baby girl home. I strapped her into her car seat and just kept smiling at her. My baby has come a long way in the past four months. I never doubted her because I knew she would make it.

"You riding with me or daddy, baby cakes?" I asked her, like she could really answer me back.

"You said daddy? Good choice," MJ smiled.

"Whatever, loser," I laughed.

"Ma cooked a whole meal fit for an army, so that's where we are headed," he said, picking up the car seat and giving me a kiss.

"Alright, I'll be right behind you. Make sure you strap my baby in right Mykell Jr.," I threatened.

"I got this mama, chill," he laughed.

"I'll make sure he does it right," Mama said, following her son.

"Thank you," I chuckled.

"So big head, how's work going?" Dad asked me.

"I love it. Actually, that is what I meant to tell you. Yesterday some light skinned chick came by there and when she noticed me she started asking questions about you. LaLa had to come out and put her in her place. As a matter of fact, it was the chick we ran into at the mall a while back."

"Damn here we go, thanks for telling me though."

"No problem, now let's go get some food and spend time with the kiddies," I joked.

When we got to the house, Amyricale and Tyriq were so excited to see Mikyah, They kept fighting over who could hold her and whose baby she was. It was so cute. Then Romell came and took her from everybody and didn't want to give her up and Mama made him.

"It's crazy how much Kamora and Mikyah look alike." Mama smiled while she held her granddaughter and I held my niece.

"I know, right? I asked MJ did he still want to get the test done and he almost cussed me out."

"Girl I tell you them Jones men don't play when it comes to their kids. They can tell if a child is theirs or not just by looking at them," she laughed.

"I'm just so happy to have my baby home, I don't know what to do."

I remember when I used to doubt my mothering abilities but now, looking into my daughter's eyes, I know I'll be the best I can be and do whatever I can to love and protect her. Unlike my mother.

Mykell

I was disturbed by the news Chyanne delivered to me about Toni questioning her about me and shit. I hadn't seen that crazy broad since we ran into her at the mall and I would have liked to keep it that way. I even went as far as to change my number so she wouldn't be able to contact me in any way. Neicey and I are in a very good place in our marriage and I'd be damned if I let anybody or anything fuck that up.

We have been through too much and it's time we get to be happy like were supposed to. I've even been thinking about renewing our vows and just starting over fresh.

I was lying in the bed with Kamora on my chest and Amyricale at my side when Neicey walked in the room. A month after she had Kamora, she'd started working at LaLa's boutique with Chyanne. She even got promoted to manager. I'm just happy she wasn't there the day Toni showed up.

"Damn, I'm jealous. You don't never hold me like that," she laughed.

"I got something you can hold," I winked at her.

"Nasty." She smiled.

"Only if you want me to be," I laughed.

"Whatever," she said, picking up Kamora and kissing all over her face.

"I got to run by the club in a minute and do some paperwork," I informed her.

She shrugged. "That's cool. LaLa was coming over anyways."

"Cool, I'm about to get ready and head out."

* * *

When I got to the club, one of the new bodyguards I had just hired named Buck was there. He was a big, black, ugly nigga.

"What's up boss?" he greeted me.

"Ain't shit Buck."

"You got a visitor in your office, she said she was your sister," he said, giving me the heads up.

I didn't even say anything else before heading straight for the elevator to see who this nigga had let in my office. I knew it couldn't be Janae or Lani because they would have just came by the house and I knew it wasn't Daniella because Neicey said she was coming over our house.

When I walked in my office, Toni was sitting behind my desk looking too comfortable for me. *What the fuck?* "What are you doing here, Toni?"

"What do you think? I came to see you. I don't appreciate you changing your number on me, then having me have to show up at your club just to see you," she said.

"Toni, take ya crazy ass on somewhere before I have to hurt you. You're a lawyer so you have to know this shit is trespassing," I said, moving to grab her out of my chair. That's when I felt her stab me in the neck with something. All of a sudden my body went numb and I couldn't talk. It was like I was paralyzed or something.

She smiled and pushed me down in my chair while unbuckling my pants. I thought was yelling for her to stop but nothing would come out. I couldn't move to get her off me so she just dropped down to her knees. "I'm tired of you denying me Mykell, enough is fucking enough," she said before taking my dick in her mouth.

I don't know if the shit felt good or not because I was still fucking numb, but the next thing I knew, I saw a fist flying and it punched her in the side of the face. Daniella and Neicey came into view. Neicey was putting a beating on Toni's ass and I was rooting for her and cheering her on even though she couldn't hear me.

"Neicey, call the ambulance quick! That bitch drugged him," LaLa screamed when she noticed the syringe.

Reneice

The only thing on my mind right then was fucking murder. I couldn't believe this bitch was trying to rape my damn husband. She was that desperate for the dick that she had to take it? Is that really how we're doing it now?

Thank God that bitch only gave him something that would temporarily paralyze him. The doctors said he should be back to his normal self in one to two days. I told MJ to look out for his brothers and sisters because I was staying here with his dad. Mykell kept feeling the need to apologize to me. Why? I don't know.

"Mykell will you stop fucking saying sorry? You don't have shit to be sorry about," I said for the tenth time.

"I'm just saying though. I don't want you trying to kill me in my sleep or something. If it makes you feel any better, I didn't even get to feel it." He smiled.

"Shut up nigga, that shit ain't funny," I laughed at his silly ass.

"Man, but yo ass hit her with a fucking Sharkeisha punch. That shit was mad crazy though."

"Oh my gosh, will you please shut up?" I shook my head.

"Alright, I'm just saying though."

"I'm just happy LaLa had to pick up something for Lakey, or else she would have succeeded and that would have been bad for you," I let him know.

"Why?" he asked.

'Because you would not have ever stuck that thing in me ever again. And I do mean *never* again," I said seriously.

"What? Man, stop playing. As a matter of fact why don't you come over here and take care of daddy real quick."

I cracked up laughing. "Never, I need to pray over that thing and we are most definitely waiting until you get tested and they come back negative."

"Aw, you playing, man"

Something on the news caught my eye so I turned it up.

Breaking news, the body of a very well-known lawyer has been found in her house burned to death. Sources say police responded to a call about a fire around 10:30 at this house behind me where criminal defense lawyer Toni Hunt lives. When firefighters were able to get inside her home, they were not able to save Ms. Hunt.

That was all I needed to hear. I was shocked because we had just seen her not even two hours ago. I looked over at Mykell and he was just as shocked as I was. We sat there trying to figure everything out until I got a phone call from LaLa.

"I took care of everything, she won't be a problem anymore," she simply said before hanging up.

What the hell?

Chapter 15

Reneice

For some reason I couldn't find my phone. I looked everywhere in this house for it but I can't seem to find it. Then all of a sudden, Mykell claimed that he had to go out of town to take care of some business but he needed to take MJ with him. I didn't even have time to question him before they walked out the door, but I guess if they wanted me to know, they would have told me what was going on.

It was lunch time at work, so I took Chyanne and LaLa out to eat, my treat. LaLa was eating like she hasn't eaten in days. Chyanne and I threw each other knowing glances. I cleared my throat to get her attention and she looked up at me with a mouthful of food.

"How far along are you and why didn't you tell me?" I asked.

She kept chewing and swallowed hard. "I just took the test at work on my break."

"So how do you feel? I knew it wouldn't be long before Lakey put one in you," I laughed.

"Neicey that's not funny. I don't know the first thing about being a mother or raising anybody. I had to raise myself because my mom couldn't do it and my dad refused to do it."

"LaLa, stop it, you're not the only one. Chyanne was scared when she found out and her mother didn't fucking help her at all, but she's doing a damn good job for her age with Mikyah. My mother passed when I was eleven and I'm doing a hell of a job raising five kids. But another thing we all have in common is we're not in this alone. We have each other and our children's fathers," I said.

She sighed. "You're right, I can do this," she smiled.

"Hell yea you can. But let me ask you something."

"Go ahead."

"What happened that night?" I asked referring to the night she killed Toni.

She smiled maliciously. "After I called the ambulance, I made sure you and Kell were straight, then I went straight to that bitch's house. See, an old friend of mine is a lawyer too, so he got her info and stuff for me. I threw some C4 that bitch way and KABOOM!" she explained.

I sat there in awe. I knew I liked her for a reason, she had a dangerous side to her and it can be very deadly. She was a no bullshit type of female and the fact that she did that for me blew me away.

"You did that for me, Daniella?" I asked.

"Duh girl, we're family right? So therefore, family looks out for family." She smiled.

"Wow," Chyanne said.

“I know, right,” I agreed.

What a hell of a day. Lakey better stick with this one, she’s a real thoroughbred chick. The definition of a ride or die.

* * *

The only sound you could hear was my black red bottom heels connecting with the concrete. I walked in the dark room to find my target strapped to the chair with his head covered. I walked over to him and took the black bag off of his face.

“So we meet again.” I smiled.

“Neicey?” he asked.

“Don’t be so surprised to see me Kamil.”

“What are you doing here?” he squirmed.

“I’m doing something I should have done a long time ago,” I said, taking my gun out. "See, not only did you fuck me over, but you also tried to hurt the one I gave my heart to. If you thought he was crazy, he ain't got shit on me. You kill for a living, but I do this shit for fun. I caught my first body before I even knew what the fuck a tampon was. All the shit I been through will make a bitch not give a fuck about anybody, I'm pretty sure you know that snitches get stitches. I'll see you in hell..."

I jumped up from my dream in a cold sweat. *He didn’t,* I thought as I ran to the other side of the room and grabbed the house phone, dialing Mykell’s number. He didn’t answer so something told me to call my phone. I did that and would you know his black ass answered. "What's up baby? You called just in time for all the fun," he said devilishly.

"Mykell, please tell me you're not doing what I think you're doing," I pleaded.

"What am I doing baby?" he taunted.

"Mykell don't play with me." I paced back and forth.

"Any last words before you go meet your maker?" I heard Mykell ask.

All of sudden my breath got caught in my chest and I couldn't breathe. Why was he doing this? How did he find him? Why do I even care? Why would he take my son with him?

BOOM! Was the last thing I heard before I dropped the phone. I sat there on floor in a daze crying silently. I can't believe he would actually kill him while I was the phone.

Mykell

I was so happy when Pops and Big Mone called and said they wanted the kids to come kick it with them for two weeks. Of course MyMy didn't want to leave her daddy, and Tyriq threw a fit about leaving Neicey, but they little asses had to go. We haven't had any time by ourselves together since our honeymoon. The only one that was allowed to stay was Kamora.

I felt really bad about killing that nigga when she was on the phone, so you know I was kissing ass hard trying to make it up to her.

The only light in the room came from the candles we had lit. I was cuddled up with the love of my life with soft music playing in the background.

“We haven’t did this in forever,” Neicey said, rubbing my curls as my head lay on her chest.

“I know, we oughtta get rid of the kids more often,” I agreed.

“Yea, but you were the one who wanted another one and we had to start all over,” she chuckled.

“I know, I always wanted five kids. Thank God we had another girl because I don’t think I would have been able to take another little me running around.”

“I’m surprised Amyricale takes to Kamora like she does. You got that little girl so spoiled and she thinks that’s her daughter, anyways.”

“I know, you be getting all jealous and shit,” I laughed.

“I do not,” She laughed.

Just then, Lyfe Jennings started singing “Must Be Nice.” I looked up at Neicey, “You remember this song?” I asked.

“Yea, this was the day I found out about Kya’s nasty ass.”

“Don’t talk bad about the dead baby, it’s not nice,” I teased.

"Whatever."

Even when you hustling days are gone

She'll be by your side still holding on

Even when those 20's stop spinning

And all those gold digging women disappear

She'll still be here

I swear he ain't never lied. He made this song was made just for me and Neicey.

"Thank you," I said.

"For what?" she asked.

"For always loving a nigga unconditionally. I don't know one woman that would have went through all the shit you did and still stick with a nigga. Even when I didn't deserve it, you still had my back. You was willing to go to prison for me all because you didn't want me to go back and that's some real shit. You might not know it but you really level me out, sometimes I wonder where I would be if you hadn't come into my life," I said sincerely.

"Well stop thinking about that because I'm not going anywhere. We in this forever, till death do us part." She kissed my lips.

Chapter 16

Micah

Mykell called me and filled me in on this surprise that he had planned for Neicey and it was hot. Not wanting to be outdone, I threw in my own little idea for a surprise I wanted to do for Janae. We gathered up the kids then headed to the airport, Pops was letting us use the private jet as always, so we headed to his spot.

I was surprised to see Ramone and his little goon squad there. He looked up at me and winked while walking towards me. He pulled me to the side so we were out of earshot. "I heard the plan and I want in, we can make this a night to remember for all of them," he said, looking behind him to make sure that the ladies weren't coming.

"That shit will be epic," I nodded my head.

"Yea and Lakey wants in on it too since LaLa is pregnant." He smiled.

"Aw man, this shit is going to be fly. I can see it now."

"Our dads are coming the day of because they didn't want to raise any suspicions. I told Lani we were just going for a visit."

"That's cool because I told Janae that Mykell needed me for something."

Hours later, we were in the Sunshine State. Kell and Lakey were there to get us when we landed. I was happy that they had brought the big boy trucks out because I don't know where we were going to fit with all these kids. We dropped the ladies and the children off at Kell's house to be with Neicey and the other kids.

We headed out to take care of some serious business. We looked for two hours before we found exactly what we each wanted. "Yea, that's the one for me," I said, looking at this pear cut diamond ring that I knew Janae would love.

We each picked out the rings we wanted then we hit up the mall to pick out our outfits for tonight. Tonight there would be three surprise engagements and one surprise re-engagement going on. They would never see this coming.

Janae

I have no idea what had gotten into Micah but he texted me earlier talking about he went shopping for me an outfit and he wanted me to look nice tonight because we're going out. I didn't know if I should be offended or what, because I always looked good, even on my off days. But if my man wanted me to look good for him, I had no objections to that.

I was really not the going out type, but I was here in Miami with my sisters, so why not? It won't hurt me to go out and enjoy myself

Lani

I found it kind of fishy that Ramone just up and told us that we were coming to Florida. He just dropped me and the girls off here then bounced. He had been gone ever since. Then he called me and told me were going out to Kell's club tonight. I had to tell him I didn't bring any clothes to be wearing to a damn club but he told me to chill out and go with the flow.

Well that's exactly what I will do. Chill out and have a good time! I got my girls with me, my brothers and my man. What could possibly go wrong?

Daniella

Ever since I told Lakey I was pregnant, his ass been on me like white on rice. I couldn't eat this, I couldn't lay like that, I couldn't wear these shoes. I felt like I was about to lose my mind! Now he's telling me we're about to go out tonight? I felt like there was a trick to it. Why would he want his pregnant girlfriend at a club? Yea, there was something definitely going on here.

Reneice

All the ladies were at my house getting ready for the night while the men were somewhere doing something. What? I don't know. They told us they were taking us out tonight but they were nowhere to be found. Marisol, our nanny, was staying in with the kids tonight but MJ and Chyanne volunteered to stay here and help her since most of the kids were under age seven.

We were all dressed to kill. See, we knew how to be sexy but classy at the same time and the dresses that our men picked were fresh to death. There was a knock at the door so I went to open it. "I have orders to take you to Laila's, safe and sound," the older white man said.

"Ladies, let's round em up!" I yelled.

When we pulled up to the club, the men were standing outside waiting on us. They all had on black suits but their shirts were the same color as our dresses. They all were looking quite handsome, if I say so myself.

"Oh my, don't you all look like y'all just stepped out of a GQ magazine," I complimented as we stepped out the truck.

"Thank you," they all said at the same time.

When we stepped in the club, the DJ was blasting Show Out by Juicy J. The girls and I immediately hit the dance floor.

Every time I go out

You know I gotta show out

Every time I go out

You know I bring that dough out

We all sang to the song while showing out on the dance floor. We danced straight through four songs until we got tired. Then we all headed to look for our men. In the middle of the hunt, the DJ cut the music in the middle of an A$AP Ferg song and played "Love and War" by Tamar Braxton.

It took me a couple of seconds to realize that she was actually in the club singing live. She was standing by the DJ's booth with the mic in her hand. Buck, the bouncer, came over and held his arm out for me to take and he led me to the front of the club where the other ladies were already standing. We were all standing there trying to figure out what was going on.

Tamar came out of the booth and walked in the front of us while still singing.

We stay on the front lines

We're still here after the bomb drops

We go so hard, we lose control

The fire starts, then we explode

When the smoke clears, we dry our tears

Only in love and war

She pointed behind us and the men were all on their knees, with ring boxes opened.

The music died down and Ramone was the first one to speak.

"Le'Lani, we have been up and we have been down. We've had some storms come our way but we eventually found our way back to each other and there is no other woman that I would want to rock my last name. You gave me two of the most beautiful daughters and I would be honored if you said you would be mine forever."

Then it was Micah's turn.

"Janae, I never knew what true love was until the day you walked into my life. You've made an honest man out of me and I wouldn't mind waking up to you for the rest of my life. I can't imagine my life without you and my kids, and I never want to find out what that would be like."

Lakey followed up after that.

"Daniella better known as my Ooh La La," he laughed. "I know we've only been at it for a little over a year but I want you to know that you rock my world. I was the type of nigga that used to be the first one to scream 'fuck love' until you came into my life. You're the first and only one to bear my kids and a wise woman once told me I better stick with you and that's what I plan to do." He winked at me.

Now it was time for my baby.

"My little firecracker, the Bonnie to my Clyde, the female version of me. You are literally my backbone, you make my world go round and I never want you out of my life. I know you heard all this before, so what I want to know is if you'll stay down with a nigga forever and marry me...again?"

"Will you marry me?" they all asked simultaneously.

"YESSSSS!" we screamed.

I ran into Mykell's arms and kissed him all over his face while the club erupted into oohs and ahhhs.

"You are so sweet." I smiled as I kissed his face.

"I know," he smiled.

We partied the rest of the night to celebrate our engagements. This was one of the best nights of my life. I never would have thought that Mykell would propose again even though were already married.

Epilogue

Two years later

Daniella

I never thought I would see the day when I would become somebody's wife, but I'm one of the happiest women in the world. Lashaun has shown me what true love is and I am very grateful for him. We have the perfect little family with our son Lashaun Marlon Mitchell, Junior, but Lakey thinks he's about to get a daughter now. we'll see about that in five years. I grew up the only child and didn't have a lot of family, but Neicey and her family welcomed me in with open arms.

I even had an opportunity to open up more boutiques here in Florida and the surrounding areas. I also decided to go back to school and get a degree in business management. Be on the lookout for me, Mrs. Mitchell.

Lakey

These niggas be out here jumping from female to female all they damn lives but that shit gets old eventually. Find you a real down ass female that you know will ride with you till the wheels fall off, then will be willing to walk with you. When you find her, settle your ass down! You can call me a sucka all you want but I love my girl and I'll be damned if I let someone else come and snatch her up because I refused to love her the way she wanted to be loved.

She and my son keep me sane around here and I been trying to get her to give me a daughter but she wanna act funny; talking about some damn five years. Yea, alright, we'll see about that.

Lani

I did it! I am officially Mrs. Le'Lani Peake. Yes, Ramone and I have been through a lot, but everything we have been through only made us stronger. I went from being in a loving relationship, then got mad because of something that Ramone did and ended up making one of the biggest mistakes of my life. It's crazy because when I first met Zamier, I never would have guessed that he liked to abuse women and had an alcohol problem.

They never lied when they said 'the grass isn't always greener on the other side'. Ladies, if you're in an abusive relationship, GET OUT! That is not love, it's actually the complete opposite. I'm just happy I made it out alive so I could spend the rest of my days with my soulmate and our kids.

Ramone

You know I had to go ahead and make my Le'Lani my wife. It was only right that I did; she's the only female that I know would put up with my bullshit and have no problems putting me in my place. She's a keeper though, I fucked up and let another nigga squeeze his bitch ass in and try to take my spot but we all knew that wasn't about to happen.

His ass put his hands on the wrong one. Nobody puts their hands on my lady and lives to tell it, never. Because of his bitch ass, I wasn't able to eat solid food for a while. That shit fucked my greedy ass up. But on a more serious note, I'm happy me and my lady decided to get it together. I love that girl with all my heart.

Micah

Who would have ever though that Mack Daddy would ever get married? Sounds crazy huh? But I found the woman that compliments me in every way possible. We were meant for each other, I don't care about what she did in her past. That shit happened before me and as long as she doesn't make the same mistakes again, we'll be cool.

I accept her for who she is, flaws and all. Nobody's past is squeaky clean, so who am I to judge her? I've done some shit in my past that I'm not proud of but that's all a part of life. You live and you learn.

Janae

That damn Micah done went and made me a housewife. It's crazy because I surely thought I had lost him when Bishop popped up, but he stuck by my side through all that bullshit. It pained me to tell him about my past and the biggest mistake I have ever made but he never judged me.

From day one, he accepted me and my daughter and I knew he was a keeper when Ranee fell in love with him. That was just a plus, now the four of us have our perfect little family and we couldn't be any better.

MJ

I became a dad at age 15 but I don't regret it. Mikyah was one of the best things that ever happened to me. Chyanne and I decided to go ahead and get the test done to put us to ease and, of course, my baby girl was 99.9% mine. She's so big and growing better than they thought she would. I remember the day she was born when I was in the hospital crying like a little bitch because she was so little. Now she's running around the house causing terror because she hit her terrible twos.

Me and Chyanne decided that since we're so young, we'll just worry about raising our daughter and getting our lives on track, then worry about being in a relationship later. We're still close and act like best friends, but we're not officially together. As long as we have our baby girl, we'll be in each other's lives.

Chyanne

Life for me is going good. I recently enrolled in college and I'm still working at the boutique. Even though MJ and I are not together, we still have a really good relationship and we do the best we can to take care of our daughter.

I even started to work on my relationship with my mother. She came crying to me one day about how she was wrong and how much she missed me. We enrolled in counseling and have been doing okay since then.

Mykell

I bet y'all didn't think we were going to make it huh? Neicey and I have been through hell and back, literally; but we beat the odds in the end and proved everybody wrong. Some of y'all didn't even think I would stay faithful once we got back together, but I proved all y'all wrong. It took me a lot of growing up to do it, but I did it and that's all that matters. As long as I have her and my kids, my life is perfect! I couldn't ask for more and I don't even think I want more. This was one crazy ass rollercoaster ride, but we survived it. Like my homie Lyfe Jennings said, 'When you got somebody good, you hold on to em.'

Reneice

We really took y'all through it huh? Just imagine how I felt. There were plenty of times that I felt like throwing in the towel and giving up, but I've never been a quitter. I knew eventually his silly ass would open his eyes and realize how much I meant to him. It took him long enough, but my baby got it together. I just want to thank you for taking the time to sit and read our story. In the end, I proved to him and everybody else that I was made to be his Official Girl.

The End

Made in the USA
Lexington, KY
15 April 2016